Getting Ahead

Communication Skills for Business English

Home Study Book

*Sarah Jones-Macziola
& Greg White*

CAMBRIDGE
UNIVERSITY PRESS

Published by the Press Syndicate of the University of Cambridge
The Pitt Building, Trumpington Street, Cambridge CB2 1RP
40 West 20th Street, New York, NY 10011-4211, USA
10 Stamford Road, Oakleigh, Melbourne 3166, Australia

© Cambridge University Press 1993

First published 1993

Printed in Great Britain
at the University Press, Cambridge

ISBN 0 521 407060	Home Study Book
ISBN 0 521 407052	Home Study Book Cassette
ISBN 0 521 448697	Home Study Book CD
ISBN 0 521 407079	Learner's Book
ISBN 0 521 407044	Learner's Book Cassette
ISBN 0 521 407036	Teacher's Guide

Copyright
The law allows a reader to make a single copy of part of a book for purposes of private study. It does not allow the copying of entire books or the making of multiple copies of extracts. Written permission for any such copying must always be obtained from the publisher in advance.

Contents

Acknowledgements	iv
How to use the *Getting Ahead Home Study Book*	1
Unit 1 Introductions and greetings	2
Unit 2 Occupations	6
Unit 3 Companies	10
Unit 4 The place of work	14
Unit 5 Progress test 1	18
Unit 6 Day-to-day work	20
Unit 7 The working environment	24
Unit 8 Plans	28
Unit 9 Visits and travel	32
Unit 10 Progress test 2	36
Unit 11 Work history	38
Unit 12 Fairs and sales	42
Unit 13 Product description	46
Unit 14 Entertaining	50
Unit 15 Progress test 3	54
Unit 16 Firms and factories	56
Unit 17 The Business Pleasure Trip	60
Unit 18 Problems, problems	64
Unit 19 Future trends	68
Unit 20 Progress test 4	72
Key and tapescripts	74

Acknowledgements

The authors and publishers are grateful to the following copyright owners for permission to reproduce copyright material. Every endeavour has been made to contact copyright owners and apologies are expressed for any omissions.

p. 10: logos reproduced by permission of Aeroflot Russian International Airlines, Bayer AG, Coca-Cola Great Britain and Ireland, Olivetti. 'Coca-Cola' is a registered trade mark of the Coca-Cola Company. p. 11: adapted questionnaire by permission of *International BusinessWeek*. pp. 26, 39, 54: adapted extracts from *The Independent on Sunday* by permission of Newspaper Publishing plc. p. 34: adapted extract from *Business Life* by permission of Premier Magazines Limited. p. 46: adapted advertisement by permission of Tulip Computers UK plc. p. 50: adapted extract, first appeared in WORKING WOMAN, December 1989. Written by Samantha Richardson. Reprinted with permission of WORKING WOMAN magazine. Copyright © 1989 by WORKING WOMAN, Inc. p54: logo reproduced by permission of Kwik-Fit (G.B.) Limited. p. 60: adapted extract, first appeared in WORKING WOMAN, June 1990. Written by Sandy Sheehy. Reprinted with permission of WORKING WOMAN magazine. Copyright © 1990 by WORKING WOMAN, Inc. p. 61 *tl*: advertisement published by permission of Dewynters plc. p. 61 *m*: advertisement reproduced by permission of The Royal Academy of Arts and R B Kitaj RA. p. 64: adapted extract from an article by Anne Ferguson in *The Independent on Sunday*, 21 April 1991, by permission of Newspaper Publishing plc. p. 68: adapted extract by permission of *The Economist*, © 1992 The Economist Publications. p. 73: adapted graph reproduced from ASIAWEEK by permission of Asiaweek Limited.

The authors and publishers are grateful to the following illustrators and photographic sources:

Illustrators: Julia Bishop-Bailey: p. 3 *tr*. Paul Chappell: pp. 6, 24, 69. Michael Ogden: p. 72. George Taylor: pp. 14, 15, 17, 22, 23, 26, 33, 34, 47, 48, 56. John York: pp. 2, 3 *m*, 62.

Cover illustration by Giovanna Pearce.

Photographic sources: BBC Photographic Library: p. 39 *tr*. Comstock Photofile Ltd: pp. 25, 38, © 1993, Comstock, Inc. Robert Harding Picture Library: pp. 12, 20, 29 *bl*. Honeywell Control Systems Ltd: p. 39 *tl*. Kwik-Fit (G.B.) Limited: p. 54. Tony Stone Photo Library: pp. 29 *br*, 60, 62. Tulip Computers UK plc: p. 46.

l = left   *r* = right   *t* = top   *m*= middle   *b* = bottom

How to use the *Getting Ahead Home Study Book*

The *Getting Ahead Home Study Book* has many activities for you to do at home. There are:
- exercises to practise grammar and vocabulary from the *Learner's Book*
- extra listening, reading and writing tasks
- test units to help you check your progress

🔑 Key

Answers to most of the exercises are in the key at the back of the book. Some exercises have no key, so compare your answers with another learner or ask your teacher to check them.

🕐 Time

Each unit has three sections; you need about twenty minutes to do a section or an hour for each unit. It is a good idea to write your answers in pencil. Then check them with the key at the back of the book. And remember, it is better to learn a little every day than a lot just before your next lesson.

👁 You

In most units there are sentences for you to complete about yourself. Try and do these, even if you do not work and are still at school or college. Learn your answers.

📼 Listening

There are two types of listening tasks in the *Getting Ahead Home Study Book*:

Listening

You listen to speakers in different business situations and answer questions or take notes on what they say. They talk at normal speed so if you cannot understand something they say, replay the tape or CD and listen again.

Listening and speaking

These tasks practise pronunciation. You listen to different speakers and repeat what they say and/or listen and reply.

There are complete tapescripts of all the listening tasks in the key. You can use these to check your answers or if you cannot understand something.

📖 Reference section

The main units finish with a reference section. This tells you about the main grammar points of that unit. There is also a list of the important words and expressions from the unit. You can write a translation in your language.

We wish you good luck and every success with the *Getting Ahead Home Study Book*.

Sarah Jones-Macziola

G Williams

UNIT 1 Introductions and greetings

1.1

1 Vocabulary

Morning, afternoon or evening? What do you say?

1 .Good morning.............

2 ....

3 ....

4 ....

2 Language in use

Read these conversations and then complete with the correct forms of the verb *to be: am, are* and *is*. Use short forms where possible, e.g. *I'm, he's.*

1 A: Good morning. I *'m*...... (1) Juan da Silva.

　B: Pleased to meet you. My name .... (2) José Hierro.

2 A: .... (3) you Ms Forgues?

　B: Yes, I .... (4). Please call me Maria.

3 A: Excuse me, ... (5) your name Shepherd?

　B: No, it .... (6). It .... (7) Fieldman.

4 A: .... (8) you Mr Xian?

　B: No, I .... (9). I .... (10) Mr Fung.

5 A: .... (11) your name Perroni?

　B: Yes, ... (12). How do you do?

6 A: .... (13) Mike Watson and Melanie Hawkes from Toronto?

　B: Yes, they .... (14).

3 Vocabulary

Match the title to the person.

1 Ms (+ family name)　　　A man
2 Mr (+ family name)　　　B married woman
3 Miss (+ family name)　　C unmarried woman
4 Mrs (+ family name)　　 D married/unmarried woman

1.2

1 Vocabulary

Look at the map and write the names of the numbered countries in the puzzle. Letters in the names make the hidden word.

Hidden word ▼

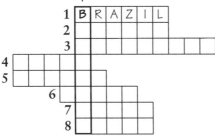

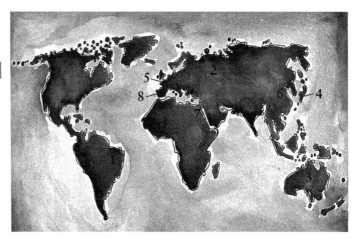

Now complete this sentence with the hidden word:

The VIP banking group has

.... in these countries.

2 Language in use

Use these phrases to complete the two conversations.

A How are you?   C Fine, thanks.   E Are you Ms Pilarski?
B My name's …   D How do you do?   F I work in …

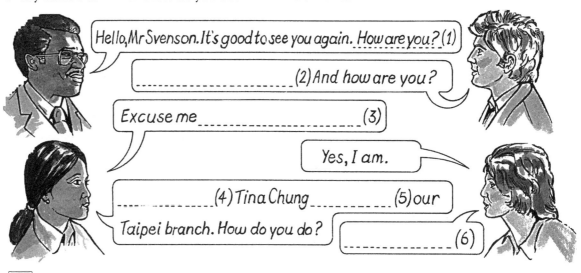

[cassette] Now listen and check your answers.

3 [cassette] Listening and speaking

Practise introductions and greetings.
First, listen and repeat like this:

Voice: Pleased to meet you.
You: (Beep) Pleased to meet you.

Now listen and answer like this:

Voice: Pleased to meet you.
You: (Beep) Pleased to meet you, too.

1.3

1 Language in use

Introduce the people in the boxes.

- Mr Tan China/Peking
- Mr Kim Korea/Seoul
- Ms Rao India/Bombay
- Mrs Manos Greece/Athens
- Mr Regueira Brazil/São Paulo
- Ms Ersoy Turkey/Istanbul

1 This is Mr Tan. He's from China. He works in the Peking office.
2 I'd like to introduce Mr Kim.
3 ....
4 ....
5 ....
6 ....

2 Language in use

Read these conversations and then complete with suitable words.

A

Warren: Hello Janette. It's .... (1) to see you again. How .... (2) you?
Janette: Not too bad. And you?
Warren: Fine, thanks. I'd like to .... (3) Paul Williams. Paul, this is Janette. She's over from Switzerland.
Paul: Hello. Nice to .... (4) you.
Janette: Nice to meet you, too.
Warren: How .... (5) some coffee?
Janette: Yes, please. Black with .... (6), please.
Paul: Same for me, too.

B

Warren: Come and meet Jodi Peterson, my assistant. Jodi, ... (7) is Janette Dupont. She's over from Switzerland.
Jodi: How .... (8) you do, Ms Dupont?
Janette: How do you do? Please .... (9) me Janette.
Jodi: And I'm Jodi. Where are you from in Switzerland?
Janette: Just outside Geneva.
Jodi: Is it your first visit to Sydney?
Janette: Yes, it .... (10).

3 Vocabulary

Fill in the missing months and days in the diary.

Now complete these sentences with your own information.

I have English classes on .... (day(s)).

My birthday is in .... (month).

THE YEAR AHEAD	THE WEEK AHEAD JANUARY
Dates to note	.... (A) 17
.... (1)	.... (B) 18
FEBRUARY	
.... (2)	WEDNESDAY 19
.... (3)	
.... (4)	.... (C) 20
JUNE	
JULY	
.... (5)	.... (D) 21
.... (6)	
.... (7)	.... (E) 22
NOVEMBER	
.... (8)	.... (F) 23

Reference section

The verb *to be*

Positive

I	'm / am	from Paris.
She / He / It	's / is	
You / We / They	're / are	

Negative

I	'm not / am not	from Tokyo.
She / He / It	isn't / 's not / is not	
You / We / They	aren't / 're not / are not	

Question

Am	I	from Athens?
Is	she / he / it	
Are	you / we / they	

Short answer

Yes,	I	am.
	she / he / it	is.
	you / we / they	are.

No,	I	'm not. / am not.
	she / he / it	isn't. / 's not. / is not.
	you / we / they	aren't. / 're not. / are not.

My name's Bob Brown. I'm from New York.
They **aren't** from Berlin, they're from Dortmund.
Are you Tom Black? Yes, I **am**.

Useful words and expressions

	Your translation
branch (noun)	....
office (n.)	....
Excuse me.	....
How do you do?	....
I'm sorry.	....
Please call me ...	....
Pleased to meet you.	....
How are you?	....
Fine, thanks.	....
Not too bad.	....
I'd like to introduce ...	....
How about some coffee?	....

UNIT 2 Occupations

2.1

1 Grammar

Fill the gaps with *a* or *an*.

1 .... accountant   3 .... secretary   5 .... supervisor   7 .... agent
2 .... clerk   4 .... engineer   6 .... manager   8 .... inspector

2 Vocabulary

Look at the pictures and choose the correct job from the words in the box.

| sales manager | engineer | sales clerk | architect | accountant | computer operator |
| bank manager | secretary | supervisor | lawyer | | |

1 .Computer operator.................

2 ....

3 ....

4 ....

5 ....

6 ....

Now write sentences about these people like this:

1 .She's a computer operator............................   4 ....
2 ....   5 ....
3 ....   6 ....

3 Listening

Listen and <u>underline</u> the number you hear.

1 12%/20%   3 13%/30%   5 50%/15%
2 2%/10%   4 80%/8%   6 66%/76%

2.2

1 Writing

These words begin with a capital letter.

1 Ms Gustafson, Mr Khartir, Mrs Iglesias, Dr Edwards
2 Toshiba, Coca Cola, Smith Exports Pty Ltd
3 Madison Avenue, Canterbury Street, World Trade Center
4 Monday, Tuesday, Wednesday
5 October, November, December
6 Mexico, Spain, Thailand

Which words above are:

A titles / people's names? ...1......
B countries? ....
C months? ....
D days? ....
E addresses? ....
F company names? ....

2 Listening

Listen and complete the address.

Horner and Horner

3 Language in use

Read these telephone conversations and then complete with suitable words.

A

Recept: Philips Exports. .... (1) morning.
Green: I'd .... (2) to speak .... (3) Mr Brown.
Recept: Who's .... (4), please?
Green: My name's Joanne Green. I'm .... (5) Colour Print.
Recept: .... (6) the line, please.
Green: Thank you.

B

Recept: Philips Exports. Good afternoon.
White: .... (7) is Ian White.
Recept: .... (8), what's .... (9) name, please?
White: White, Ian White. Can I .... (10) to Mrs Black, please?
Recept: Just a .... (11).
White: .... (12).

2.3

1 Listening and speaking

Practise asking questions about people.
First, listen and repeat like this:

Voice: What's his surname?
You: *(Beep)* What's his surname?

Now listen and answer like this:
Voice: What's his surname?
You: *(Beep)* His surname's Sirotto.

Note: Use the information on this business card to help you answer the questions about Alex Sirotto.

ALEX SIROTTO
Product Manager

GIZMO GADGETS LTD

Prospect Place
Swindon
Tel: 0793 626315
Fax: 0793 626350

---

2 Language in use and listening

Some information is missing from this woman's business card. What questions can you ask to find out more information about her?

1 What's her first name?
2 ....
3 ....
4 ....
5 ....
6 ....

.... (1) .... (2)
Accountant

.... Inc. (3)

....
Boston, Mass (4)
Tel: .... (5)
Fax: .... (6)

Now listen and fill in her business card.

3 Writing

Complete these sentences about yourself.

I work for .... (*company*)
    as .... (*position*).
My business address is ....
My business telephone number is ....
My private address is ....
My private telephone number is ....

Reference section

Articles

an + vowel	a
	e
	i
	o
	u
a + consonant	

He's **an** architect.
She's **a** lawyer.

Pronouns

Subject	Object
I	me
you	you
she	her
he	him
it	it
we	us
they	them

What does **he** do?
What's **her** phone number?

Possessive adjectives

my
your
her
his
its
our
their

Cardinal numbers

1	one	11	eleven	21	twenty-one
2	two	12	twelve	30	thirty
3	three	13	thirteen	40	forty
4	four	14	fourteen	50	fifty
5	five	15	fifteen	60	sixty
6	six	16	sixteen	70	seventy
7	seven	17	seventeen	80	eighty
8	eight	18	eighteen	90	ninety
9	nine	19	nineteen	100	a/one hundred
10	ten	20	twenty	1000	a/one thousand

Useful words and expressions

Your translation

What do you do? ....

Who do you work for? ....

I'd like to speak to … ....

Speaking. ....

Hold the line, please. ....

Who's speaking? ....

List the jobs which are important to you and your work.

....

....

....

....

....

....

....

UNIT 3 Companies

3.1

1 Vocabulary

Complete these sentences with the correct nationality.

1 Lucky Goldstar is a .... *Korean* .... company.
2 BMW and VW are .... companies.
3 KLM is a .... airline.
4 Volvo and Saab are .... companies.
5 JAL is a .... airline.
6 AT&T is an .... multinational company.

Can you add some more nationalities to these groups?

-ese	-ish	-(i)an
Portuguese	*Spanish*	*Russian*
....	....	....
....	....	....

2 Vocabulary and listening

Can you match the company headquarters to the places?

1 Coca Cola   A Moscow
2 Bayer   B Ivrea
3 Olivetti   C Atlanta
4 Aeroflot   D Leverkusen

Now listen and give the correct headquarters like this:

Voice: The headquarters of Coca Cola are in New York.
You: *(Beep)* No, they're not. They're in Atlanta.

3 Writing

A customer wants some information about your electronics company. What can you tell them? Use the information in the box to help you.

1 I work for ....
2 We're a .... company.
3 Our headquarters ....
4 We have branches ....

Name:	Higgins Electronics
Nationality:	British
Headquarters:	Glasgow
Branches:	New York, London and Frankfurt

This company is one of your competitors. What can you tell your customers about them? Use the information in the box to help you.

5 One of our competitors is ....
6 They ....
7 Their ....
8 ....

Name:	Total Electronics
Nationality:	Taiwanese
Headquarters:	Taipei
Branches:	San Francisco, London and Tokyo

3.2

1 Vocabulary

Service or manufacturing industries? Write [S] or [M].

1 [S] transport   4 [ ] clothing   7 [ ] banking
2 [M] vehicles   5 [ ] aerospace   8 [ ] chemicals
3 [ ] insurance   6 [ ] engineering   9 [ ] tourism

2 Reading

Fill in this card with information on your own company or a company you know well.

INTERNATIONAL BUSINESSWEEK

May 20, 199-   This card must be received by July 22, 199-

PLEASE PRINT
Name ....
Business ....
[ ] Business   [ ] Home   Address ....
....
City ....
Country ....
Postal Code ....
Fax Number ....

Please check one response for each following question.
1 What is your company's type of business?
MANUFACTURING
1 [ ] Food/Drink/Tobacco 2 [ ] Textiles/Clothing 3 [ ] Engineering
4 [ ] Chemicals 5 [ ] Vehicles 6 [ ] Other manufacturing –
please specify ....
SERVICES
1 [ ] Import/Export 2 [ ] Hotels 3 [ ] Telecommunications
4 [ ] Travel/Transport 5 [ ] Banking 6 [ ] Insurance 7 [ ] Accounting
8 [ ] Legal 9 [ ] Other services –
please specify ....
2 What is your title?
A [ ] General Manager B [ ] Division Manager C [ ] Department Manager
D [ ] Other Manager E [ ] Student F [ ] Other –
please specify ....
3 How many employees are there in your company worldwide?
1 [ ] Under 100 2 [ ] 100–999 3 [ ] 1,000–2,499 4 [ ] 2,500–4,999
5 [ ] 5 000–9,999, 6 [ ] 10,000 or more

3 Grammar

Complete these questions with *is, are, do* or *does*.

1 .... American Express in the insurance business?
2 What .... Fuji sell?
3 .... Seat and Skoda make cars?
4 .... Pepsi and Coca Cola in the banking business?
5 What .... IBM and Apple produce?
6 .... Toyota produce computers?

Now match the questions to these answers.

A Computers. .5.......   C No, it doesn't. ....   E No, they aren't. ....
B Yes, it is. ....   D Photographic equipment. ....   F Yes, they do. ....

4 Writing

Complete these sentences about your own company or a company you know well.

I work for .... (*company*).
We're in the .... (*business*).
We produce .... (*goods*).
Our customers are .... (*companies*).
Our competitors are .... (*companies*).
We export to .... (*countries*).

3.3

1 Language in use

Match the questions to the answers.

1 Where are your headquarters?   A Chips.
2 What's your turnover?   B Worldwide.
3 Who are your competitors?   C Tokyo, Japan.
4 What do you produce?   D IBM, Intel.
5 Where do you export to?   E 100,000.
6 How many people do you employ?   F $18 billion.

2 Reading and listening

Read this information on AFL. Then make questions to find out the missing information.

AFL

Sales of $..................... (1), ... (2) employees. Production and sales in over 200 companies around the world. That's AFL today.

AFL tomorrow – we expect strong growth in our main businesses: .... and .... (3). We have .... (4) subsidiaries in the .... and in .... (5).

AFL today and tomorrow. In a position to solve problems in food supply, environmental protection and energy recovery.

1 What ....?
2 How many ....?
3 What ....?
4 How many ....?
5 Where ....?

Now listen to someone talking about AFL and fill in the missing information.

Reference section

Present simple tense

Positive

I You We They	make sell export	widgets.
She He It	makes sells exports	

Negative

I You We They	don't do not	make sell export	widgets.
She He It	doesn't does not		

Question

Do	I you we they	make sell export	widgets?
Does	she he it		

Short answer

Yes,	I you we they	do.
	she he it	does.

No,	I you we they	don't. do not.
	she he it	doesn't. does not.

> We **make** clothing.
> They **don't export** to China.
> **Does** Volvo **sell** cars? Yes, it **does**.

Useful words and expressions

	Your translation		Your translation
branch (n.)	....	export (verb)	....
competitor (n.)	....	import (v.)	....
customer (n.)	....	make (v.)	....
employee (n.)	....	manufacture (v.)	....
headquarters (n.)	....	produce (v.)	....
subsidiary (n.)	....	sell (v.)	....

List the industries and services that are important to you and your work.

....
....
....
....
....
....
....

UNIT 4 The place of work

4.1

1 Vocabulary

Look at the building and write sentences to say where the departments are.

1 .Reception is on the ground floor..
2 After-Sales ....
3 The canteen ....
4 .... is on the first floor.
5 Accounts ....
6 Production ....
7 .... is on the sixth floor.
8 .... is on the fourth floor.
9 The Managing Director's office ....

Note: ground floor (BE) / first floor (AE); canteen (BE) / cafeteria (AE)

2 Language in use

Look at this plan and complete the conversations.

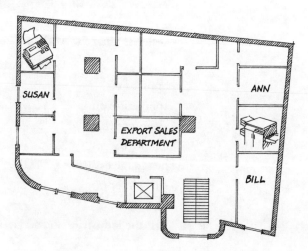

A

A: I'm looking for a photocopier.
B: Go up the stairs to the second floor. Go straight along the corridor and the photocopying room is the .... (1) door on the .... (2). It's .... (3) Ann and Bill's offices.

B

A: I need to send a fax.
B: .... (4) up the stairs to the second .... (5). At the stairs .... (6) left. The fax machine is the .... (7) door on the .... (8). It's .... (9) Susan's office.

3 Writing

Complete these sentences with information about your colleagues or other people you know.

.... works in Accounts.
.... works in Personnel.
.... works in ....
.... works in ....

4.2

1 Vocabulary

Complete these sentences. Then write the missing words in the puzzle below and find the hidden word.

1. R & D .... new products.
2. Personnel deals with ....
3. Accounts deals with ....
4. and 5 Marketing .... and .... the company's products.
6. Purchasing buys .... for the company.
7. Production .... the company's products.
8. Sales .... the company's products.
9. Dispatch .... the goods to customers.
10. After-Sales helps .... with problems.

Hidden word ▼

	1	D	E	V	E	L	O	P	S

Now complete this question with the hidden word:

Which .... do you work in?

2 Vocabulary

Match the documents in the box to the pictures.

catalogue
order form
price list
cheque
invoice
c.v.

1 ....   3 ....   5 ....

2 ....   4 ....   6 ....

3 Reading

Read this letter.
What enclosures will you send?
Fill in the numbered gaps.

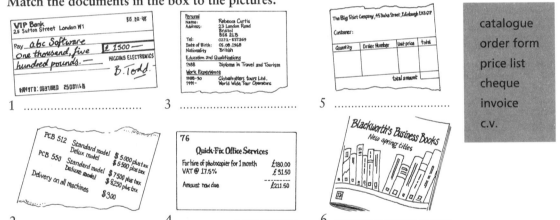

KIDSWEAR, PO Box 43, Watford WD4 5TX, England
Tel 0923 55675
Fax 0923 79583

Mr F Haupt
Der Kinderladen
Marktplatz 5
6020 Innsbruck
Austria

30 August 199-

Dear Mr Haupt

Thank you for your enquiry of 23 August about our range of children's clothing.
I enclose some information which I hope you will find of interest. Please contact me if I can be of any further help.

Yours sincerely

Roberta Sinclair

Enc: .... (1)
     .... (2)
     .... (3)

4.3

1 Language in use

Read these conversations and then complete with suitable words.

A

Barroso: This is Juan Barroso. .... (1) you put me .... (2) to Mrs Williams in the Sales .... (3)?

Recept: I'm afraid she's .... (4) a meeting. Can I .... (5) a message?

Barroso: Yes, please. Can you ask .... (6) to call me back?

Recept: Of .... (7). Who's .... (8) please?

Barroso: Juan Barroso. And my number is 356 3583.

B

Paretti: My name's Maria Paretti. Could you .... (9) me with Jonathan Andrews in Production?

Recept: I'm sorry, but he's .... (10) a customer at the moment. .... (11) I take a .... (12)?

Paretti: Yes, please. Can you .... (13) him to call .... (14) back?

Recept: .... (15). .... (16) calling, please?

Paretti: Maria Paretti.

2 Vocabulary and listening

Which departments deal with these items? Can you match them?

1 customers' orders   A Personnel
2 invoices   B After-sales
3 problems with goods   C Sales
4 job advertisements   D Accounts

Now listen and ask for the correct department like this:

Voice: I'm calling about my order number 384.
You: (Beep) Could you put me through to the Sales department?

3 Listening

Listen to this phone call and fill in the phone message form.

```
              Phone Message

For:    ........................................

From:   ........................................

Of:     ........................................

Phone:  ........................................

Message: .......................................

        ........................................
```

Reference section

Ordinal numbers

1 first	11 eleventh	21 twenty-first
2 second	12 twelfth	30 thirtieth
3 third	13 thirteenth	40 fortieth
4 fourth	14 fourteenth	50 fiftieth
5 fifth	15 fifteenth	60 sixtieth
6 sixth	16 sixteenth	70 seventieth
7 seventh	17 seventeenth	80 eightieth
8 eighth	18 eighteenth	90 ninetieth
9 ninth	19 nineteenth	100 hundreth
10 tenth	20 twentieth	

Prepositions

next to   opposite   between   on the right   on the left

Useful words and expressions

                                                  Your translation

corridor (n.)

lift (BE) / elevator (AE)

enclosure (n.)

floor (n.)

stairs (n.)

I'm looking for …

on the right

Could you connect me with …?

Could you put me through to …?

Certainly.

Of course.

I'm afraid she's …

Can I take a message?

Can you ask her to call me back?

Who's calling, please?

List the departments that are important to you and your work.

UNIT 5 Progress test 1

5.1 Grammar

Complete these sentences with the correct form of the verb in (brackets). Use short forms if possible.

Gina and I .....work............ (work) (1) for Eurobags. Gina .... (be) (2) a marketing assistant and I .... (be) (3) a sales clerk. She .... (work) (4) in Marketing and I .... (work) (5) in Sales.
Eurobags .... (be) (6) an Italian company. The headquarters .... (be) (7) in Traviso, but we .... (have) (8) subsidiaries in Brazil and Venezuela. Eurobags .... (be) (9) in the packaging business. It .... (produce) (10) paper and plastic shopping bags. Its main markets .... (be) (11) in Europe, but it also .... (export) (12) to the US and South America.

5.2 Grammar

Write short answers to these questions.

1. Are you an accountant?
   .No, I'm not...............
2. Does American Express have a branch in your country?
   Yes, ...
3. Is Seat a French company?
   No, ...
4. Do you produce camcorders?
   Yes, ...
5. Do you export to the US?
   No, ...
6. Does your company sell office equipment?
   Yes, ...

5.3 Grammar

Fill in the correct preposition (*at*, *in* or *on*).

1. He's .... vacation.
2. I work .... Citicorp.
3. Mrs Agnelli's office is .... the fourth floor.
4. I'm afraid she's .... a meeting.
5. She's .... lunch.
6. He's .... a business trip.

5.4 Language in use

On the right there are some statements. What do you say first?

1. .Pleased to meet you....................................... Pleased to meet you, too.
2. .... Not too bad, thanks.
3. .... I'm an engineer.
4. .... Yes, please. Black with sugar.
5. .... Mr Tan's office is on the right.
6. .... You're welcome.

5.5 Vocabulary

Underline the word which is different from the others in each group.

1 Italian, Japanese, France, Swedish
2 secretary, branch, engineer, clerk
3 Marketing, Accountant, Sales, Research and Development
4 third, first, eighth, ten
5 headquarters, chemicals, engineering, tourism
6 Monday, February, Sunday, Friday

Now add some more words to each group.

1 ....
2 ....
3 ....
4 ....
5 ....
6 ....

5.6 Language in use

Read this telephone conversation and then complete with suitable words.

You: Good morning .... (1).
Caller: This is Gina Lee from Harris International.
You: I'm sorry, ... (2)?
Caller: Gina Lee from Harris International. I'd like to speak to Mr Salomon.
You: I'm afraid .... (3).
Caller: Oh. Well, could you put me through to Mrs Steffan?
You: She's .... (4)?
Caller: Yes, please. Can you ask her to call me back?
You: .... (5)?
Caller: It's 866 3659.
You: .... (6).
Caller: Thank you. Goodbye.

5.7 Listening

Read this telephone message. Then listen to the phone call and check if the numbered information in the message is correct. Write any corrections to the message below.

David

Please call Mark Taylor (1) on 0648 49684 (2) about your order for 50 typewriters (3). It is not very urgent (4).

Sue

1 ....
2 ....
3 ....
4 ....

UNIT 6 Day-to-day work

6.1

1 Listening

Listen to Ana Campos talking about her working times and write true [T] or false [F] for each sentence.

1 She starts work at 7.30. [ ]
2 She finishes work at 4.00. [ ]
3 She has lunch at 12.00. [ ]
4 She has 45 minutes for lunch. [ ]
5 She works a 40-hour week. [ ]
6 She doesn't work on Friday afternoon. [ ]

flexitime: a system of flexible working hours

2 Vocabulary

Look at the words in the box and put them into groups.

at	on	in
..nine o'clock..........	..Monday.................	..July.....................
....	....	....
....	....	....

nine o'clock   Monday
July   12.30
the morning   summer
lunchtime   1997
1 May   Friday
Tuesday morning   noon

Now complete these sentences with the correct preposition.

1 We start work .... 8.30 and finish .... 4.00.
2 What time do you finish work .... Friday afternoon?
3 Do you have a break .... the afternoon?
4 The next meeting is .... 3 April.

3 Reading

Read this article about working times in Holland, Japan and Sweden and write the names of the countries on the charts.

The formal working week is 40 hours, but the average Swede clocks up only 37. On a typical day, one in every four workers is not in the office or factory. Of this 25% about 10% are sick and the other 15% are looking after children, on study leave or on holiday. Swedish workers have 28 days' holiday.

The average Japanese worker spends 47 hours a week, or 2,100 hours per year, at the office or factory. Only 30% work a five-day week. The Japanese have 15 days' paid holiday, but many workers take only half of that.

The average Dutch worker works a 34-hour week. This is not because Holland's workforce is lazy. One quarter of the workforce is part-time, more than twice the number in Japan. Dutch workers also take five weeks' paid holiday.

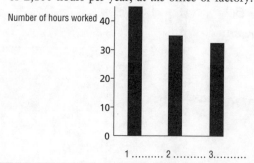

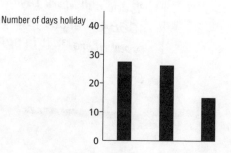

6.2

1 Grammar

Complete these questions with *do* or *does* and words from the box.

have	get	do	start	leave	have

1 How ......do..... you .....get.... to work?
2 What time .... you .... work?
3 Where .... you .... lunch?
4 How long .... you .... for lunch?
5 When .... your boss .... the office?
6 What .... you .... in the evening?

Now match the questions to these answers:

A An hour. ...4.....   C I read the paper or watch television. ....   E At nine o'clock. ....
B By train. ....   D In the canteen. ....   F I don't know. ....

2 Listening and speaking

A friend phones you to tell you about their new job. Unfortunately the line is bad and you can't understand everything. Listen and ask questions like this:

Voice: I go to work by ...
You: (*Beep*) I'm sorry, how do you get to work?

3 Grammar

Put the words in (brackets) in the correct place in the sentence. Write the sentences on a separate sheet of paper.

1 I make phone calls (*often*).

   .I often make phone calls...............

2 I meet customers (*hardly ever*).
3 My boss goes on trips (*three times a year*).
4 The Sales Department entertains visitors (*once a month*).
5 I work late (*sometimes*).
6 We go to meetings (*often*).
7 Do you read the *Financial Times* (*every day*)?

4 Writing

Complete these sentences about yourself.

I get up at ....
I normally go to work/college by ....
I usually arrive at college/my workplace at ....
In the morning I ....
In the afternoon I ....
On a normal day I finish work/college at ....
After dinner I ....
I go to bed at ....

6.3

1 Reading

Read these advertisements and then fill in the missing information in the table.

	A	B
Salary	£12,000	
Hours		
Holidays		
Other Benefits		

A

MARKETING TRAINEE
£12,000 per annum

Staff benefits include: six weeks' annual holiday, free lunches, bonus payment after 12 months and flexitime working a 35-hour week. If you are available to start in early September, please write with a full C.V. to:
Pamela Beaty, Human Resources

B

Terms of employment include 24 days' annual leave, flexible working hours and a salary of £19,494. Applications, together with a full C.V. should be sent to:
The Personnel Manager

2 Vocabulary

Complete these sentences. Then write the missing words in the puzzle below and find the hidden word.

1 The people you work with are your ....
2 The person you work for is your ....
3 Do you usually have lunch in the ....?
4 How many days' .... do you get a year?
5 The night .... starts at 10 p.m.
6 Another word for (4) is ....
7 Do you have an .... job?
8 How many .... a week do you work?
9 It takes me an hour to get to work. It's a terrible ....
10 The basic .... is £15,000 a year.

Hidden word ▼

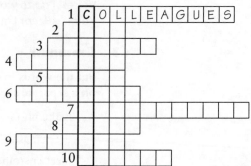

1: C O L L E A G U E S

Now complete this sentence with the hidden word:

This puzzle is about working ....

3 Vocabulary and grammar

Which verbs go with which words?

1 go on   A late
2 make   B the computer
3 work   C a business trip
4 work with   D a report
5 go to   E a meeting
6 write   F phone calls

Fiona Wilson works in Marketing. What does she like doing, and what doesn't she like? Look at these pictures and write six sentences about her on a separate sheet of paper. The first one is done for you.

1 *She likes going on business trips.*

Reference section

Time

You say the time like this:

09.35 = nine thirty-five
     = twenty-five to ten

Note: a.m. = in the morning
       p.m. = in the afternoon or evening

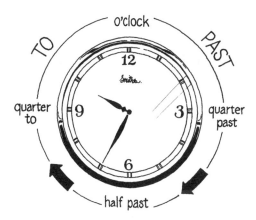

Prepositions of time

at	+ time	I start work **at** nine o'clock.
on	+ day + date	I don't work **on** Sundays. The meeting is **on** 23 March.
in	+ month + year	I usually go on holiday **in** August. I joined the company **in** 1990.

Word order of adverbs

I You We	always often never	work late.

I You We	work late	once a week. twice a month. three times a year.

> I **never** start work before ten o'clock.
> He's **often** late for work.
> We go on business trips **twice a year**.

Useful words and expressions

	Your translation
always (adverb.)	....
normally (adv.)	....
usually (adv.)	....
often (adv.)	....
sometimes (adv.)	....
hardly ever (adv.)	....
rarely (adv.)	....
never (adv.)	....
boss (n.)	....
colleague (n.)	....
flexitime (n.)	....
hours (n.)	....
perks (n.)	....
salary (n.)	....
shift (n.)	....
hate (v.)	....
like (v.)	....
mind: I don't mind (v.)	....

UNIT 7 The working environment

7.1

1 Vocabulary

Complete these sentences with the correct form of *make* or *do*.

1 Marie usually .... the coffee.
2 Paulo .... the filing.
3 Henri .... photocopies.
4 Julie .... a lot of phone calls.
5 Pascal never .... overtime.
6 Marcelle .... appointments for the boss.

2 Language in use

Look at the pictures and ask people to do things. The first request is done for you.

1 Could you spell your name, please?
2 ....
3 ....
4 ....
5 ....
6 ....

3 Listening and speaking

Practise asking people to do things and answering them.
First, listen and repeat the requests like this:

Voice: Could you spell 'personnel', please?
You: (*Beep*) Could you spell 'personnel', please?

Now listen and answer like this:

Voice: Could you spell 'personnel', please?
You: (*Beep*) Sure. That's P.E.R.S.O.N.N.E.L.

Note: There are no correct answers. Use your own information to answer the requests!

7.2

1 Listening

Listen to Armel Dubois talking about his new job. Then answer yes [Y] or no [N] to these questions.

Does he have to:
1 work long hours? [ ]
2 travel? [ ]
3 go to conferences? [ ]
4 visit customers? [ ]
5 take his holiday in August? [ ]
6 write a monthly report in English? [ ]

2 Grammar

You are talking to a new colleague about your working environment. Study the examples in the Reference section and then complete these sentences with *mustn't* or *needn't*.

1 You ...mustn't... smoke in the factory.

2 You .... be in the office before eight a.m.

3 You .... park in the boss's parking space.

4 You .... wear a suit to the office.

5 You .... wear jeans to meetings.

6 You .... make personal phone calls at work.

3 Writing

Complete these sentences about yourself with *have to* or *don't have to*.

I .... work hard.

I .... do overtime.

I .... work long hours / study a lot.

I .... travel a lot.

I .... go to conferences.

I .... speak English in the office / at college.

7.3

1 Reading

Read this article and match the paragraphs to the pictures.

How to lead a better life

........A Get regular fresh air. Sunshine is cheering, rain refreshing. Best of all, fresh air gets you out of the office. Most offices are unhealthy.

........B Get out of your car and onto public transport. You will reduce noise, get fitter and have more time to read, think and look.

........C Don't travel long distances to work. Find a job near home. Move out of the city.

........D Go home from work earlier. Long hours don't make you more efficient. If there's too much work for you to do, say so.

........E Learn to enjoy yourself. Relax, play sport or music, take up a hobby. Please yourself more – make/find time to do it.

........F Exercise regularly, eat sensibly, don't smoke or drink alcohol, cut down on caffeine drinks. Try water or herbal teas.

2 Language in use

What advice can you give for these problems? Use *should, shouldn't* or *Why don't you …?*.

1 I'm always late for work.
   Why don't you get up early?

2 I'm always tired.
   ....

3 It takes me two hours to get to work.
   ....

4 My boss wants me to learn English.
   ....

5 I can't sleep.
   ....

6 My colleague smokes non-stop.
   ....

Reference section

Modal verbs

Positive

I You She He It We They	can could must should	work on Saturday.

Negative

I You She He It We They	can't cannot		work on Sunday.
	could must should	n't not	

Question

Can Could Must Should	I you she he it we they	work on Saturday?

Short answer

Yes,	I you she he it we they	can. could. must. should.	No,	I you she he it we they	can't. couldn't. mustn't. shouldn't.

Useful words and expressions

Your translation

Asking people to do things:
Could you …?   ....
Would you …?   ....

Telling people it is necessary to do things:
You have to …   ....
You must …   ....

Telling people it is not necessary to do things:
You don't have to …   ....
You needn't …   ....

Note: mustn't tells people **not** to do things.

Giving advice:
You should …   ....
You shouldn't …   ....
Why don't you …?   ....

extension (n.)   ....

Not at all.
No problem.   ....

I'd rather not.   ....
It's rather urgent.   ....
Sure.   ....

It takes (me) an hour …   ....

UNIT 8 Plans

8.1

1 Grammar

Look at Mr Lee's diary for next week and write some sentences about his plans.

Monday	Wednesday
Attend the Sales and Marketing conference	a.m. Meet production manager p.m. Visit new factory
Tuesday	**Thursday**
Have lunch with Ann	a.m. Finalize sales contract p.m. Go to the Computer Fair

1 He's attending the Sales and Marketing conference on Monday.
2 ....
3 ....
4 ....
5 ....
6 ....

2 Vocabulary

Today is Wednesday. Match the day on the left to the phrase on the right.

1 Thursday   A tonight
2 Wednesday afternoon B the day after tomorrow
3 Wednesday evening   C yesterday
4 Saturday   D tomorrow
5 Friday   E in three days' time
6 Tuesday   F this afternoon

3 Writing

What are your plans and arrangements for next week?

....
....
....
....
....
....

8.2

1 Grammar

A customer is coming on a business trip to your country. Write questions asking about her plans. Use the words in (brackets) to help you.

1 *(When/arrive?)* When are you arriving?
2 *(Where/stay?)* ....
3 *(Which companies/visit?)* ....
4 *(How long/stay?)* ....
5 *(Who/see?)* ....
6 *(When/leave?)* ....

2 Listening and speaking

You phone Mr Zuckermann's secretary about his visit to your company. It's a very bad line and you can't understand everything. Ask questions like this:

Secretary: He's arriving at ... o'clock.
You: (*Beep*) I'm sorry, when's he arriving?

3 Language in use

Read this telephone conversation and then complete with suitable words.

Arbose: Hello. Is .... (1) Andy Brecker?

Brecker: Yes, ... (2).

Arbose: It's Connie Arbose here. .... (3) are you?

Brecker: Not too bad. What about you?

Arbose: Oh, I'm .... (4). Listen, I'd like to .... (5) a meeting for next week. Are you .... (6) on Tuesday?

Brecker: I'm .... (7) not. I'm going to Head Office then.

Arbose: Well, ... (8) .... (9) Wednesday?

Brecker: No, that's no good. We've got a sales meeting. But I'm free .... (10) Friday. Does Friday .... (11) you?

Arbose: Yes, I'm not doing anything on Friday. Early afternoon. Is two o'clock OK?

Brecker: Yes, that's fine. .... (12) you on Friday at two.

8.3

1 Vocabulary

Complete these sentences. Then write the missing words in the puzzle below and find the hidden word.

1 Am I .... at the Holiday Inn again?
2 You're .... the ten o'clock flight from JFK airport.
3 When am I .... dinner with the agent?
4 Am I .... the production team?
5 Is the sales manager .... the fair?
6 Are we having .... with the other agent?
7 You're .... to Dallas on Friday morning.
8 You're .... Dallas on Saturday.

Hidden word ▼

1	S	T	A	Y	I	N	G

Now complete this sentence with the hidden word:

This is my .... for next week.

2 Listening

A secretary is making appointments for her boss, Diana Dinkel. Listen to the phone calls and write the appointments in the diary.

These are the callers:
1 Maria Rodriguez
2 Rich Calder

9 Monday
11.30 Planning meeting
2.00 Sales team

10 Tuesday
....
....

11 Wednesday
10.30 Steve Morgan
2.30 Mr Gardini

12 Thursday
....
....

13 Friday
....
....

3 Writing

Rewrite this fax with the correct punctuation and layout. Use a separate sheet of paper.

june 3 199-

dear mr gardini i am writing to confirm your appointment with ms dinkel on wednesday june 11 at 2.30 in ms dinkels office best regards marita collins

Reference section

Present progressive tense with a future meaning

Positive

I	'm	going	to the conference.
She He It	's	flying	
You We They	're		

Negative

I	'm not	going	to the conference.
She He It	isn't	flying	
You We They	aren't 're not		

Question

Am	I	going	to the fair?
Is	she he it	flying	
Are	you we they		

Short answer

Yes,	I	am.
	she he it	is.
	you we they	are.

No,	I	'm not. am not.
	she he it	isn't. 's not. is not.
	you we they	aren't. 're not. are not.

We use the present progressive to talk about future appointments and arrangements:

> What **are** you **doing** on Monday?
> **I'm attending** a conference.

Useful words and expressions

	Your translation
conference (n.)	....
diary (n.)	....
trade fair (n.)	....
arrange (v.)	....
arrive (v.)	....
attend (v.)	....
catch (v.)	....
depart (v.)	....
leave (v.)	....
meet (v.)	....
visit (v.)	....
Are you free on (*Friday*)?	....
How about (*the afternoon*)?	....
I'd like to …	....
Does (*Tuesday*) suit you?	....
I'm afraid not.	....

UNIT 9 Visits and travel

9.1

1 Vocabulary

Look at the words in the box and put them into groups.

Business	Travel	Weather
presentation	journey	fine
...	...	...
...	...	...
...	...	...

journey
presentation
fine   wet   flight
overcast
conference   trip
windy   trade fair
meeting

2 Grammar

Read this conversation and then complete with *was, wasn't, were, weren't, did* or *didn't*.

Eicher: Hello, Ms Peres. It's good to see you again. Let me help you with your bag.
Peres: Thanks very much.
Eicher: How .... (1) the flight?
Peres: Fine, fine. A bit long.
Eicher: When .... (2) you leave Panama City?
Peres: Well, it .... (3) foggy, so the flight .... (4) delayed.
We .... (5) leave until ten a.m. local time.
Eicher: Oh, really? .... (6) there any stopovers?
Peres: No, there .... (7). It .... (8) a direct flight.
Eicher: .... (9) you sleep on the plane?
Peres: No, I .... (10).
Eicher: You must be tired. I'll drop you off at your hotel.

3 Reading

Read this article and fill in the missing information in the chart. What percentage of visitors come for business and what percentage for a holiday?

International travel and tourism is big business

In 1950 there were 25 million international travellers and their business was worth about US$ two billion. Now there are over 400 million international trips every year, worth over US$200 billion.

In the last ten years there was over a 100% increase in the number of people visiting Australia. In the early 80s there were about 900,000 visitors each year. By the start of the 90s there were over two million. The pie chart on the right shows the percentage of visitors by their country of residence. The largest group were Asian, the second largest group of visitors were from New Zealand, 23% were from Europe and 19% were from the Americas.

The main reason people came was for a holiday. Over half the visitors were in this category. Another important reason was visiting relatives. This was why 21% of the visitors came. Business was the reason for 13% of the visitors and 12% of the visitors were on their way to another country.

Visitors to Australia: countries of residence

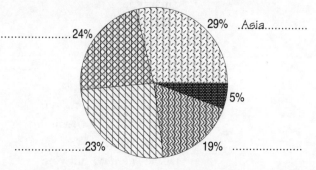

29% Asia
24%
5%
23%
19%

9.2

1 Grammar

Your colleague was at this conference. Ask questions about the trip. Use the words in (brackets) to help you.

1 (*conference?*) What was the conference like?
2 (*hotel?*) ....
3 (*food?*) ....
4 (*speakers?*) ....
5 (*other people?*) ....
6 (*weather?*) ....

Now match the questions to the answers.
A They were very friendly. .5.......
B It was terrible. It was cold and wet. ....
C It was awful. Hamburgers and fries. ....
D Some of them were very good. ....
E It was very noisy. It was next to a building site. ....
F It wasn't very interesting. ....

International Medical Conference in Hawaii

June 10-14

Guest speaker:
Dr Hiroshi Yamamoto

✱Five-star hotel✱

✱International cuisine✱

✱Five mins from beach✱

2 Listening and speaking

Listen and repeat the questions like this:

Voice: What was the conference like?
You: (*Beep*) What was the conference like?

3 Grammar

Ask more questions about the conference like this:

1 (*enjoy/conference?*) Did you enjoy the conference?
2 (*stay/Hilton?*) ....
3 (*meet/Dr Yamamoto?*) ....
4 (*go/a lot of workshops?*) ....
5 (*learn/anything?*) ....
6 (*have/good time?*) ....

Now match the questions to the answers.

A No, I didn't. It was too expensive. .2.......
B No, not really. It was disappointing. ....
C Yes, I did. But not at the conference. ....
D No, I didn't. He didn't come. He was ill. ....
E Yes, I did. But they weren't very interesting. ....
F No, nothing new. ....

4 Listening and speaking

Listen and repeat the questions like this:

Voice: Did you enjoy the conference?
You: (*Beep*) Did you enjoy the conference?

9.3

1 Reading

Read this article about airport hotels and write the headings in the correct places.

A Up-to-date flight departure information
B Fast reception and check-out
C Frequent airport transport
D Something to do in the evening
E Good restaurants
F Reliable message service

What makes a good hotel?

1 *Frequent airport transport*
If you have to wait an hour for the hotel bus at the airport or you miss your flight the next morning because the bus is late, it is not a service. It's a disaster.

2 ....
Everyone wants to arrive and to leave at the same time. Nobody wants to stand in a line to register when they are tired or to pay the bill when they are in a hurry.

3 ....
In a city hotel, you can go out to that nice little restaurant around the corner. In an airport hotel, you eat their food or go hungry.

4 ....
Nobody wants to rush to the airport check-in desk and wait for two hours when you could stay in your hotel room.

5 ....
If an important message for you gets lost when you are at an airport hotel, you can be in the wrong continent by the time you find out.

6 ....
Being alone in a strange hotel isn't much fun. Live entertainment is great. If not, a choice of videos or a movie channel can make the evening enjoyable.

2 Listening

Listen to a guest registering at a hotel. Write true [T] or false [F] for each sentence.

1 She wants a room for two nights. [ ]
2 A single room costs £85 a night. [ ]
3 Breakfast is from eight to ten. [ ]
4 She can't phone Korea from her room. [ ]
5 She can send a fax from the business centre. [ ]
6 She wants to pay by American Express. [ ]

Reference section

Past tense of the verb *to be*

Positive and negative

I / She / He / It	was / wasn't / was not	busy.
You / We / They	were / weren't / were not	

Question

Was	I / she / he / it	busy?
Were	you / we / they	

Short answer

Yes,	I / she / he / it	was.
	you / we / they	were.

No,	I / she / he / it	wasn't. / was not.
	you / we / they	weren't. / were not.

Past tenses of other verbs

Question

Did	I / you / she / he / it / we / they	fly?

Short answer

Yes,	I / you / she / he / it / we / they	did.

No,	I / you / she / he / it / we / they	didn't. / did not.

> **Did** you **leave** London on Friday? Yes, I **did**.
> **Did** he **meet** the sales manager at the trade fair? No, he **didn't**.

Useful words and expressions

	Your translation
business (n.)	....
on business	....
exhibition (n.)	....
meeting (n.)	....
seminar (n.)	....
trade fair (n.)	....
training course (n.)	....
crowded (adjective)	....
excellent (adj.)	....
disappointing (adj.)	....
fantastic (adj.)	....
pleased (adj.)	....
productive (adj.)	....
stressful (adj.)	....
successful (adj.)	....
terrible (adj.)	....
tiring (adj.)	....
useful (adj.)	....
What was it like?	....

UNIT 10 Progress test 2

10.1 Grammar

Fill in the correct form of the verb in (brackets). Use short forms where possible.

Last week I .was.......... (be) (1) at a fair in Munich, but my assistant .... (not come) (2) with me. She .... (be) (3) on holiday.

Next week I .... (go) (4) on another business trip. This time my assistant .... (come) (5) with me. We .... (fly) (6) to Brussels and I .... (stay) (7) at the Grand Hotel. First we .... (go) (8) the trade fair and then we .... (meet) (9) some customers. After that I .... (have) (10) dinner with friends, but my assistant .... (not come) (11) with me. She .... (catch) (12) the evening flight home.

10.2 Grammar

Make sentences from these words.

1 a week once have we a meeting sales
   .We have a sales meeting once a week.......................
2 the reports my boss prepares usually
   ....
3 rarely nine phone calls he makes before o'clock
   ....
4 I twice on business trips go a year
   ....
5 meets clients you day every do?
   ....
6 we normally to the sales go conference
   ....

10.3 Grammar

Complete the questions to match the answers.

1 What ....?
  I'm an accountant.
2 Who ....?
  I work for a Japanese company.
3 How ....?
  I drive.
4 Where ....?
  In a little restaurant near my office.
5 When ....?
  I finish work at seven o'clock.
6 What ....?
  I go jogging or meet friends.

10.4 Grammar

Complete these sentences with *at*, *in*, or *on*.

1 My flight is .... half past four.
2 Is there a meeting .... Monday?
3 The next workshop is .... 31 July.
4 Do you go home early .... Friday afternoons?
5 I make important phone calls .... the morning.
6 Do you mind working .... the weekend?

10.5 Language in use

Write suitable replies to these sentences.

1 Did you have a good flight?
   ....
2 Are you doing anything tomorrow?
   ....
3 I've got too much work.
   ....
4 Could you work late this evening?
   ....
5 What was the weather like in Seoul?
   ....
6 Would you copy this report, please?
   ....

10.6 Vocabulary

Write the opposite of the word underlined.

1 I finish work at six.   .....start...............   4 When are we leaving Madrid? ....
2 The conference was boring. ....   5 The flight was early.   ....
3 I never get to the office   .... 6 The service was excellent.   ....
  before nine.

10.7 Language in use

Read this telephone conversation and then complete with suitable words.

Customer: Sales department. Good morning.
You: ....(1)
Customer: Speaking. How are you?
You: ....(2)
Customer: A meeting? Sure. When?
You: ....(3)
Customer: Wednesday? I'm afraid I can't make Wednesday. We've already got a meeting then.
You: ....(4)
Customer: Yes, that's fine.
You: ....(5)
Customer: Goodbye.
You: Goodbye.

10.8 Listening

Barbara Pike is going on a business trip. Listen to her asking a colleague for information about the country and mark the correct answer.

1 Where's the Welcome Inn?
   a) in the city centre
   b) near the airport
   c) in the suburbs
2 What's the best way to get from
   the airport to the city centre?
   a) train
   b) taxi
   c) bus
3 When do the banks open?
   a) 7.30
   b) 8.30
   c) 9.30
4 When do the shops close on Saturdays?
   a) 4.00
   b) 5.30
   c) 6.30
5 What's the weather usually
   like at this time of year?
   a) warm
   b) cold and dry
   c) cold and wet
6 When is she going on the business trip?
   a) the middle of this month
   b) the fifth of next month
   c) the fifteenth of next month

UNIT 11 Work history

11.1

1 Grammar

Complete this list of irregular verbs.

Present tense	Past simple tense	Present tense	Past simple tense
am	....	have	....
is	....	....	got
are	....	go	....
become	....	leave	....
....	began	....	said
....	came	....	stole
do	....	take	....
		....	thought

2 Grammar

Read the text. Then fill in the gaps with the correct form of the past simple. Choose from the verbs in the box.

| be   be not   begin   have   be   get   go   think   turn |

château: a French castle
four-star: high quality

What do you do if you have a château on the west coast of France and no money to maintain it? Mme de la Sablière *wasn't*.......... (1) short of ideas. She .... (2) on a management course, ... (3) a bank loan and .... (4) the château into a four-star hotel with a top chef. When she .... (5), many people .... (6) she .... (7) mad. Ten years later she .... (8) a turnover of eight million francs and the restaurant .... (9) very successful.

3 Reading and listening

These sentences are a summary of Mr Van der Linde's career. Put them into the correct order.

A Took a management course after he left Unilever. [ ]
B Got his first job at Unilever. [ ]
C The bank lent him money to start a business. [ ]
D Worked for Unilever for five years. [ ]
E Two months after he got the bank loan he left Philips. [ ]
F Finished studying in 1974. [1]
G Left Unilever in 1979. [ ]
H Joined Philips in 1981. [ ]
I Set up his own business. [9]

 Now listen to Mr Van der Linde talking about his career and check your answers.

11.2

1 Reading

Read these two texts and answer the question.

Dennis Kennedy

Dennis Kennedy, 55, was born and educated in Scotland, where he trained as an engineer. He began his industrial career with Honeywell, the controls system manufacturer, in 1960. He moved to GEC and then on to ITT for 13 years. He worked in the US and different countries in Europe. In 1982 he ran Veeder Root and then moved to Qume Corporation, both in America. Finally he returned in 1989 to Britain and Honeywell. In January 1990 he took over as chairman and managing director, and is vice-president of Honeywell, Europe.

Sir John Harvey-Jones

Sir John Harvey-Jones, 66, began his career in the Royal Navy, where he interpreted Russian and German. He joined ICI when he was 32, and became chairman in 1982. Sir John retired from ICI in 1987. However, he didn't give up work. He published a book, *Making it Happen*, and presented the BBC's television programme *Troubleshooter*. He divides his time between charities, education, business and public speaking and is chair of *The Economist* magazine.

Who did these things? Fill in Dennis Kennedy [DK] or Sir John Harvey-Jones [HJ].

1 [DK] studied in Scotland.
2 [ ] started his career as an interpreter.
3 [ ] worked for ICI.
4 [ ] worked for ITT.
5 [ ] became chairman of a company in 1990.
6 [ ] wrote a book.
7 [ ] worked for the same company until he retired.
8 [ ] lived and worked in many different countries.

2 Vocabulary

Look at the phrases in the box and put them into groups.

> lived in the USA   worked for six months   took a course in marketing
> can speak three languages   studied accountancy   got a job at IBM   has computer skills
> trained as a bank clerk   can type   learned French   worked for ABB   joined JVC

Education	*Work experience*	*Other information*
took a course in marketing	worked for six months	lived in the USA
....	....	....
....	....	....
....	....	....

3 Listening and speaking

You meet someone at a party. He tells you about his career, but the party is noisy and you can't hear everything. Listen and ask questions like this:

Voice: I joined the company in 19 ...
You: (*Beep*) I'm sorry. When did you join the company?

11.3

1 Vocabulary

These sentences describe past jobs. Read them and put them into the correct boxes. 1 and 2 are done for you.

1 I did a lot of overtime.
2 The work was very interesting.
3 We had flexitime.
4 I learnt a lot.
5 I didn't get on with my boss.
6 I had a lot of holiday.
7 I worked with interesting people.
8 I worked shifts.
9 I had a lot of contact with my colleagues.
10 It was well paid.
11 There was an excellent canteen and a sports club.
12 It was hard work.

Hours	People	Work	Other
1,		2,	

2 Vocabulary

Find phrases in the exercise above with a similar meaning to these sentences.

1 I liked my colleagues.   I worked with interesting people.
2 The work was very demanding.   ....
3 The training was excellent.   ....
4 I often worked at night.   ....
5 The facilities were very good.   ....
6 I often worked late.   ....

3 Writing

Complete these sentences about yourself.

I was born in .... (*place*).
I went to school in .... (*place*).
When I left school I .... (*training*).
After that I ....
My first job was as a .... (*position*).
Now I work as a .... (*position*).

Reference section

Past simple tense

Regular verbs

	Spelling rules
train +-ed = tra**ined**	Add -ed to words except:
live +-ed = li**ved**	words ending in -e: add -d live + -d = lived
study +-ed = stud**ied**	words ending in consonant + -y: change **y** to **i** and add -**ed** study + -**ed** = stud**ied**
plan + -ed = plan**ned**	words ending in a vowel + consonant: double the consonant and add -**ed** plan + -**ed** = plan**ned**

Irregular verbs

leave – left
go – went
get – got
take – took
come – came
become – became
begin – began

We use the past simple to talk about past events. We often use it with these time expressions:

> yesterday
> last week, last month
> two months **ago**, six years **ago**
> **in** July, **in** 1986
> **when** I joined the company

Useful words and expressions

	Your translation
career (n.)	....
c.v. (curriculum vitae) (BE) / résumé (AE) (n.)	....
education (n.)	....
experience (n.)	....
qualification (n.)	....
training (n.)	....
join (*a company*) (v.)	....
leave (*a company*) (v.)	....
move (*to another department*) (v.)	....
recommend (*someone*) (v.)	....
study (*economics*) (v.)	....
go on / take a course in (*computing*) (v.)	....
train as (*a sales clerk*) (v.)	....
I would be grateful ...	....
I wonder if you could help me?	....

UNIT 12 Fairs and sales

12.1

1 Listening

Listen and write down the dates you hear.

A .... C ....

B .... D ....

2 Listening and speaking

Listen and answer the questions like this:

Voice: When does the trade fair start?
You: (*Beep*) On the second of February.

```
1  02.02
2  04.12
3  01.01
4  22.04
```

Use the dates in the box to answer the questions. *Note*: the month is the second number!

3 Grammar

Look at these notes on the International Language Show and make questions like this:

International Language Show

1 Stands near entrance?
2 Cheap accommodation near Centre?
3 Good restaurants near Centre?
4 Shops near Centre?
5 Parking near Centre?
6 Sporting events at weekend?

1 .Are there any stands near the entrance?...

2 ....

3 ....

4 ....

5 ....

6 ....

Now match these answers to the questions above.

A I'm afraid not. But there are some near the cafeteria. ....1...

B No, there isn't. It's better to take a cab. ....

C Yes, there are. There's a tennis tournament on Sunday. ....

D Yes, there are some excellent restaurants nearby. ....

E No, there aren't. But there's a shopping centre downtown. ....

F Yes, there is. The Park Hotel isn't too expensive. ....

12.2

1 Vocabulary

Complete these sentences. Then write the missing words in the puzzle below and find the hidden words.

1 I'm .... in your cycling equipment.
2 We have a wide .... of mountain bikes.
3 This one is .... in two colours.
4 We can .... from stock.
5 The .... is $299.
6 I'd like some .... about your products.
7 This is our .... model.
8 We can offer a .... of 10% on large orders.
9 Would you like a ....?

Hidden words ▼

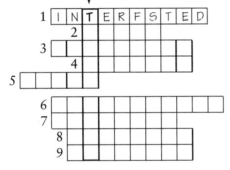

Now complete this question with the hidden words.

When did you last go to a .... ?

2 Listening and speaking

You are at a trade fair. The salesperson is telling you about their new product but the fair is noisy and you can't hear everything. Listen and ask questions like this:

Voice: This model costs ...
You: (Beep) I'm sorry, how much does it cost?

3 Writing

Complete these sentences with information about your company's product, or a product you know well.

We make/sell/distribute .... (product).
It's popular with .... (customers).
It sells well in .... (countries).
It's suitable for .... (use).
It's available in .... (colours/sizes/etc.).
It costs .... (price).
We can usually deliver .... (time).

12.3

1 Reading

Complete this letter with words from the box.

Dear Customer

We .... (1) a copy of our latest catalogue: you will note that we have increased the number of .... (2) on offer.

All of the items are currently in .... (3), but if an item you require is out of stock and not .... (4) for the next 14 days, we will .... (5) you.

Please make sure you put your telephone number on the .... (6).

Yours sincerely

order
enclose
contact
products
stock
available

2 Reading

Look at this catalogue from the Big Shirt Company and answer the questions.

T-SHIRTS in six colours. Material: 50% cotton, 50% polyester. All one size.

Pink	W21 765 13	Green	W21 765 18		
White	W21 765 23	Black	W21 765 28		
Blue	W21 765 33	Yellow	W21 765 38		
Quantity	25	50	100		
Price	£9.75 each	£9.45 each	£8.95 each		

SWEATSHIRTS Material: 100% cotton.

White	W21 970 054		
Quantity	20	50	100
Price	£18.95 each	£17.95 each	£16.95 each

SWEATSHIRTS Material: 100% cotton.

Blue	W21 970 058	Black	W21 970 062
Quantity	20	50	100
Price	£20.50 each	£19.50 each	£18.50 each

1 How many colours are the T-shirts available in? ....
2 Are they available in different sizes? ....
3 What is the unit price if you order 25 T-shirts? ....
4 How much do 100 T-shirts cost? ....
5 What is the order number for the white sweatshirts? ....
6 Are the sweatshirts available in black? ....

3 Listening

A customer is placing an order for items from the Big Shirt Company's catalogue. Listen and complete the information on the order form.

The Big Shirt Company
45 Duke Street, Edinburgh EH3 6TP

Customer:

Qty	Order Number	Unit Price

Reference section

Days of the week

Sunday
Monday
Tuesday
Wednesday
Thursday
Friday
Saturday

Months of the year

January   July
February   August
March   September
April   October
May   November
June   December

You say dates like this:

01.08.1999 = the first of August nineteen ninety-nine (BE)
08.01.1999 = August first nineteen ninety-nine (AE)

Some and any

Positive

| There's **some** ... |
| There are **some** ... |

Negative + question

| There isn't **any** ... |
| There aren't **any** ... |
| Is there **any**...? |
| Are there **any**...? |

Countable nouns

| a room | singular |
| some rooms | + plural |

Uncountable nouns

| some accommodation | no plural |

Useful words and expressions

	Your translation
discount (n.)	....
price (n.)	....
size (n.)	....
weight (n.)	....
cotton (n.)	....
leather (n.)	....
man-made (n.)	....
nylon (n.)	....
It's suitable for (*children*).	....
It's popular with (*business people*).	....
It's available from (*stock*).	....

Add some more colours to this list:

yellow

....
....
....
....
....

UNIT 13 Product description

13.1

1 Vocabulary

Match the adjectives in the first column to the opposite adjectives in the second column like this:

1 new   A small
2 good   B slow
3 fast   C short
4 quiet   D difficult
5 long   E bad
6 cheap   F old
7 big   G noisy
8 easy   H expensive

2 Reading

Read this advertisement for Tulip computers. Then answer the question.

We could have made a bigger, slower, uglier machine for around £1,000 more.
But the competition beat us to it.

All computers aim to offer power at affordable prices. Some are more successful than others. Here are some facts about the Tulip dc. Use them to make a few comparisons and save a lot of money.

Tulip's dc is a very reliable machine. This is because we use high quality components and operate strict test procedures. It is also faster, cooler and more reliable than other computers and comes in a smaller box. You can see how slim it is.

What does it offer you?

The Tulip dc has every feature you'd expect of a high quality machine, some pleasant surprises and some free bonuses. These include software, a mouse and as much service and support as you will ever need.

The Tulip dc costs £1,695. Compare this to the competition: The Deskpro Model 40 from Compaq Computer Corporation at £2,585 and the PS/2 model from International Business Machines at £2,918. Don't pay more for less. For more details call our Sales Support Department on 0800 521146.

Tulip Computers
The name for European quality.

Are these statements about the Tulip dc true [T] or false [F]?

1 The Tulip dc is smaller than similar computers. [ ]
2 It is not as fast as similar computers. [ ]
3 It is more reliable than the competition. [ ]
4 Service and support is included in the price. [ ]
5 The Deskpro 40 isn't as cheap as the Tulip dc. [ ]
6 The PS/2 is more expensive than the Tulip dc. [ ]

13.2

1 Grammar

These adjectives are all in the Tulip advertisement in 13.1. Complete the lists.

Adjective	Comparative	Superlative
big	bigger	the biggest
cool	....	....
fast	....	....
reliable	....	....
slow	....	....
....	smaller	....
successful	....	....
....	uglier	....

2 Vocabulary and writing

Which adjectives go with which nouns?

1 high   A discount
2 long
3 short   B delivery time
4 small
5 low   C price
6 large

You want to buy some dictaphones. Look at these notes on the different suppliers and write some sentences about them.

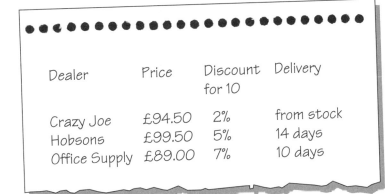

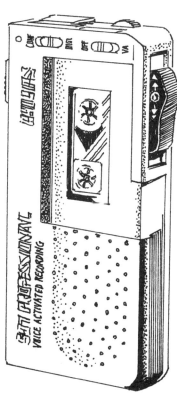

1 Crazy Joe ..has the smallest.............................. discount.
2 Hobsons .... price.
3 Hobsons .... delivery time.
4 Office Supply .... price.
5 Office Supply .... discount.
6 .... the best offer.

13.3

1 Vocabulary

Match the words in the box to the pictures.

| photocopier   bookcase   shelves   filing cabinet   calendar   map   fax machine   typewriter |

1 .... 3 .... 5 .... 7 ....

2 .... 4 .... 6 .... 8 ....

2 Language in use

What suggestions can you make for these problems? Use the words in the box to help you.

1 These chairs aren't very comfortable.
   I think we should ...buy some new chairs..............................

2 There's nowhere to keep all these papers and documents.
   Let's ....

3 I never know when it's time for lunch.
   We could ....

4 I don't know where all our branches are.
   ....

5 It's very difficult to phone Tokyo.
   ....

6 I never know what day of the week it is.
   ....

| chairs   map   clock |
| filing cabinet   calendar |
| fax machine |

3 Listening and speaking

You sell office furniture. Practise giving information about prices like this:

Voice: How much are the large size desks?
You: (Beep) One hundred and twenty-nine pounds.

Now you try. Use this price list to help you.

Office Furniture

Desks
– standard size £95.00
– large size £129.00

Tables
– office table £55.00
– reception table £42.50

Storage
– filing cabinet £150.00
– cupboard £247.50
– bookcase £69.50

Chairs
– typist £81.00
– executive £183.00

Reference section

Comparisons and superlatives

Short adjectives

Adjective	Comparative	Superlative	Spelling rules
cheap	cheaper	the cheapest	+ -er; + -est
wide	wider	the widest	+ -r; + -st
big	bigger	the biggest	+ consonant + -er: + -est
busy	busier	the busiest	-y + -ier; + -iest

Long adjectives

Adjective	Comparative	Superlative
modern	more modern	most modern
important	more important	most important

Irregular adjectives

Adjective	Comparative	Superlative
good	better	best
many/much	more	most
bad	worse	worst

They are different:

> The desktop computer is **cheaper than** the portable computer.
> The portable computer is **more expensive**.
> The mainframe computer is **the most expensive**.

They are the same:

> The portable computer's warranty is **as long as** the desktop's.

Useful words and expressions

	Your translation
equipment (n.)	....
furniture (n.)	....
guarantee (n.)	....
maintenance (n.)	....
service contract (n.)	....
warranty (n.)	....
cheap (adj.)	....
expensive (adj.)	....
fast (adj.)	....
high (adj.)	....
large (adj.)	....
long (adj.)	....
low (adj.)	....
modern (adj.)	....
short (adj.)	....
slow (adj.)	....
small (adj.)	....
wide (adj.)	....
Let's …	....
I think we should …	....
We could …	....

UNIT 14 Entertaining

14.1

1 Reading

Look at these statements about business people and social customs. Then read the article from an American business magazine. Are the statements true [T] or false [F]?

1 It's the end of the year. You receive a lot of party invitations from sales people. Reply only to the invitations you want to accept. [ ]
2 Your party invitation is for eight o'clock. You should arrive at half past eight. [ ]
3 You get to the restaurant but your host isn't there. Wait at the bar and have a drink. [ ]
4 At the party, talk to your host about politics. [ ]
5 Your host tries to sell you her latest product. Suggest a meeting for next week. [ ]

The good (business) guest's guide

The RSVP rule

It's the end of the year and your desk is full of invitations to lunches and dinners from advertising agencies, stationery suppliers and other sales people. Which do you reply to? All of them. But you don't have to agree to attend all of them.

Invitations to cocktail parties for new product lines go to hundreds of people. So only go if your company is interested in the new product. But if one of your biggest suppliers sends you an invitation to a party celebrating the tenth anniversary of your business relationship, reply immediately. If you're not sure you can go, call and explain your situation; perhaps the company can arrange another time.

How to get there

It's essential to arrive at business functions at the correct time. If you arrive at a restaurant before your host, wait at the bar. Your host will pick up the tab for your drink.

Small talk tips

Your host will try to get to know you better by asking you where you were born, where you went to school, your interests etc. It may seem like small talk, but now is your chance to find out about the supplier's background and products — all good information for future business. If your host tries to sell you her latest product, suggest you talk next week. But if you are unhappy with the service, let her know that things could be better.

RSVP: please reply to the invitation   small talk: social conversation   bill (BE) / tab (AE)

2 Language in use

Match the questions on the left to the answers on the right.

1 Where are you from?   A Tennis and golf.
2 What do you do?   B Yes please. An orange juice.
3 Is it your first visit to the USA? C Yes, I am.
4 Are you interested in sport?   D I'm in advertising.
5 What sports do you play?   E Melbourne, Australia.
6 Can I get you a drink?   F Yes, it is.

3 Listening and speaking

Practise asking people questions and answering them.

First, listen and repeat like this:

Voice: Where are you from?
You: *(Beep)* Where are you from?

Now listen and answer like this:

Voice: Where are you from?
You: *(Beep)* I'm from ...

Note: You should use your own information.

14.2

1 Language in use

Read these telephone conversations and then complete with suitable words.

A

Ross: Hello, Karen. This is Sam Ross .... (1). How are you?
Beck: Fine. Nice to hear you.
Ross: I'd like to .... (2) you to lunch next week.
Beck: That's very .... (3) of you. When exactly?
Ross: Does Wednesday .... (4) you?
Beck: Yes, that's .... (5). What time?
Ross: Is one o'clock all right? At the Holiday Inn?
Beck: Yes, that's fine. I'll look .... (6) to it. Bye.
Ross: Bye.

B

Ross: Hello, Don. It's Sam Ross here. I'm meeting Karen Beck for .... (7) next week. Would you .... (8) to join us?
Lohr: That .... (9) nice. When .... (10)?
Ross: Wednesday. At one o'clock at the Holiday Inn.
Lohr: Oh, I'm afraid I can't .... (11) Wednesday. I've got to go down to the factory then.
Ross: That's a .... (12).
Lohr: Thank you for asking me, anyway.
Ross: Another time. Bye.
Lohr: Bye.

2 Writing

This is your diary for next week. Look at these invitations and write a reply to each one. Use a separate sheet of paper. The first one is done for you.

Monday	11.00–3.00 sales meeting
Tuesday	20.00 concert
Wednesday	
Thursday	finish sales report
Friday	12.30 lunch with sales rep

1 Ms Lazarony is visiting us on Monday. Would you like to join us for lunch?
   I'm afraid I can't make Monday. I've got a sales meeting.
2 How about a game of tennis on Monday evening?
3 Are you doing anything on Tuesday evening? We're going to an Indian restaurant.
4 I'd like to invite you to lunch next week. Does Wednesday suit you?
5 How about meeting for lunch next week? Are you free on Thursday?
6 Would you like to have a drink on Friday after work?

3 Writing

Rewrite this letter with the correct punctuation and layout. Use a separate sheet of paper.

> mary simmons
> bodycare inc
> 111 park avenue south
> new york ny 10003
>
> july 10 199-
>
> dear mary thank you for your letter of july 4 inviting me to attend the launch of your new range of bodycare products i am pleased to accept and look forward to seeing you on august 7 best regards
>
> *janice*

14.3

1 Vocabulary

Fruit or vegetables? Write [F] or [V].

1 [V] pepper   5 [ ] strawberry
2 [ ] banana   6 [ ] orange
3 [ ] melon   7 [ ] carrot
4 [ ] mushroom   8 [ ] cherry

Now write the names of some vegetables and fruits you like.

Vegetables: ....

Fruit: ....

Write the names of three vegetables and three fruits you don't like.

Vegetables: ....

Fruit: ....

2 Listening

Listen to this conversation in a restaurant. What does the man order?

1 ....
2 ....
3 ....

Menu

Starters	Cucumber soup
	Prawn cocktail
	Stuffed mushrooms
Main Course	Beef Strogonoff
	Lamb Shaashlik
	Chicken Kiev
	All dishes are served with rice, baked potatoes or French fries.
Desserts	Fresh strawberries and cream
	Fruit salad
	Ice cream
	Coffee
	or
	Cheese and biscuits

3 Writing

Complete these sentences with your own information about food you know.

.... is a local speciality.
.... is very popular here.
.... is a kind of vegetable.
.... is (a bit) like ....
.... is/are very hot.
.... is quite rich.
.... is quite sweet.
.... is very spicy.

Reference section

Useful words and expressions

	Your translation
dessert (n.)	....
dish (n.)	....
guest (n.)	....
host (n.)	....
main course (n.)	....
menu (n.)	....
starter (n.)	....
invite (v.)	....
invitation (n.)	....
local restaurant	....
Does (*Monday*) suit you?	....
It would be a pleasure.	....
I can't make (*Friday*).	....
I'll look forward to it.	....
That sounds nice.	....
That's a pity.	....
That's fine.	....
That's very kind of you.	....
Would you like to …?	....
When exactly?	....
It's a kind of (*fruit*).	....
It's like …	....

15 Progress test 3

15.1 Grammar

Fill in the correct past tense form of the verb in (brackets).

Tom Farmer .... (*leave*) (1) school when he .... (*be*) (2) 15 and .... (*get*) (3) a job with a local tyre firm. At 20 he .... (*join*) (4) Goodyear as a salesman. At 24 he .... (*start*) (5) his own business. He .... (*sell*) (6) this four years later and .... (*go*) (7) to the USA. But at 31 he .... (*come*) (8) back to the UK to start a motor vehicle business called Kwik-Fit which now has a turnover of £193 million.

15.2 Grammar

Here are the answers to some questions. What are the questions?

1 When ....?
   I joined the company six years ago.
2 What ....?
   I was an office assistant.
3 Which ....?
   I worked in After-sales.
4 How long ....?
   I worked in that department for 18 months.
5 ....?
   Yes, we have some rooms free.
6 ....?
   No, we don't have any T-shirts in stock.

15.3 Grammar

Complete these sentences with the correct comparative or superlative form of the adjective in (brackets).

1 A typewriter is .... (*cheap*) than a computer.
2 IBM is the .... (*big*) computer company in America.
3 A notebook computer is .... (*expensive*) than a desktop one.
4 I think a desktop computer is .... (*good*) than a notebook one.
5 In my opinion, a telephone is the .... (*important*) piece of office equipment.
6 The .... (*fast*) way to contact a client is by phone.

15.4 Grammar

Complete these sentences with a suitable word.

1 The trade fair is .... June.
2 It starts .... June 19.
3 I'm interested .... your range of office equipment.
4 This model is very popular .... Europe.
5 It's available .... three sizes.
6 It's not really suitable .... young children.

15.5 Language in use

Write a suitable response to these sentences.

1 Would you like to meet for lunch on Monday?
....
2 Did you enjoy your first job?
....
3 Could I speak to someone in the Accounts department?
....
4 How about a portable phone for the office?
....
5 What would you like as a main course?
....

15.6 Vocabulary

Add some more words to each list.

1 Office furniture: chair, ...
2 Fruit: orange, ...
3 Colours: black, ...
4 Materials: plastic, ...

15.7 Language in use

Read this telephone conversation and then complete with suitable words.

Ass: Sales department. Good morning.
You: ....(1)
Ass: Certainly. What exactly would you like to know about our filing cabinets?
You: ....(2)
Ass: They cost $199 each.
You: ....(3)
Ass: I'm sorry, but they're not available in black.
You: ....(4)
Ass: We can deliver by the end of the week.
You: ....(5)
Ass: You're welcome. Thank you for calling.

15.8 Listening

Read this information from an office supplier's catalogue. Then listen to a phone conversation between a customer and the supplier. Is the numbered information in the catalogue correct?

1 ....
2 ....
3 ....
4 ....
5 ....
6 ....

from $63.00 [1]
8001 Very good quality typist chair, gas lift, fully adjustable, rounded front seat. Black or grey from stock [2]. Colours are an extra $9 [3] with blue or red from stock.

from $101 [4]
3005 Very comfortable and practical operator's chair. Gas lift height adjustment. Black or grey from stock [5]. Colours are an extra $11 [6] with blue or red from stock.

UNIT 16 Firms and factories

16.1

1 Language in use

Read these conversations and then complete with suitable words.

A

Visitor: My name's Tibor Petrenkó. I've got an .... (1) with the Production Manager.

Porter: You .... (2) this badge for security. And .... (3) you .... (4) the visitor's book, please?

Visitor: Yes, ... (5) .... (6).

B

Man: It's very noisy in the .... (7). Now, it's .... (8) not to touch the machinery. Please .... (9) this way.

C

Man: Right. I think that's everything. Is there anything .... (10) you'd like to .... (11)?

Visitor: Thank you. That was very .... (12).

2 Vocabulary

Which words go together?

1 Be   A out!
2 Watch   B back!
3 Stand   C touch!
4 Don't   D careful!

Now look at these pictures and write the correct warning under each one.

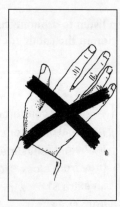   

1 .... 2 .... 3 .... 4 ....

16.2

1 Grammar

Complete this table of irregular verbs.

Infinitive	Past tense	Past participle
be	was/were	been
buy	....	....
come	....	....
....	....	done
get	....	....
go	....	....
have	....	....
....	left	....
make	....	....
meet	....	....
....	....	put
....	said	....
see	....	....
sell	....	....
....	....	spoken
read	....	....
take	....	....
write	....	....

2 Writing

Mr Cox is personal assistant to Mr Bly. Look at his 'To do' list for his boss's trip.
Write questions about his list like this:

1 .Have you booked a flight?......................... [ ]
2 .... [ ]
3 .... [ ]
4 .... [ ]
5 .... [ ]
6 .... [ ]

> **To do**
>
> Mr Bly's trip to Chicago
>
> 1 book flight
> 2 reserve hotel room
> 3 arrange meeting with Gruber
> 4 change meeting with Klonowski
> 5 confirm meeting with Gruber
> 6 cancel meeting with Pinkowski

Now listen to a conversation between Mr Bly and Mr Cox and tick the things Mr Cox has done.

3 Writing

What have you done this week? Write some sentences. Use the verbs in the box to help you.

1 .... late for work/college.
2 .... a day off.
3 .... home early.
4 .... English.
5 ....a letter.
6 .... a phone call.

be	go	make
speak	read	
take	write	

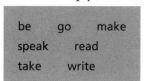

16.3

1 Vocabulary

Reread the American Pasta Corporation's company report on page 92 of the *Learner's Book*. Then complete these sentences and write the missing words in the puzzle below to find the hidden word.

1 We've increased ....
2 We'ver invested in new ....
3 Another word for factory is ....
4 We've acquired another ....
5 Rigoletto is the leading .... in New York.
6 We've installed a new pasta drying ....

Hidden word ▼

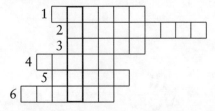

Now complete this sentence with the hidden word:

You can read about all these things in the annual ....

2 Grammar

Make sentences from these words to give news for a company report. Don't forget to use the past simple with time phrases!

1 (open/office/Seattle)
   We've opened an office in Seattle.
2 (close/factory/Atlanta)
   ....
3 (start/exporting/Japan)
   ....
4 (start/exporting/Japan/last year)
   ....
5 (sell/popcorn business)
   ....
6 (buy/frozen food company)
   ....

3 Listening and speaking

A friend phones you with news of their company. Unfortunately the line is bad and you can't understand everything. Listen and ask questions like this:

Voice: We've opened an office in ....
You: (*Beep*) I'm sorry, where have you opened an office?

Reference section

Present perfect tense

Positive

I You We They	've have	been there. done that.
She He It	's has	

Negative

I You We They	've not haven't have not	been there. done that.
She He It	's not hasn't has not	

Question

Have	I you we they	been there? done that?
Has	she he it	

Short answer

Yes,	I you we they	have.
	she he it	has.

No,	I you we they	've not. haven't. have not.
	she he it	's not. hasn't. has not.

We use the present perfect to give news and talk about changes. When something happened is not so important.

We've installed a new computer system.

We often use it with these time expressions: **just   recently   yet   already**

If we want to say when something happened, we use the past simple (see Unit 11).

We installed a new computer system last year.

Useful words and expressions

	Your translation
Be careful.	....
Don't touch.	....
Stand back.	....
Watch out.	....
Have you phoned him yet?	....
I've just phoned her.	....
brand (n.)	....
company report (n.)	....
market research (n.)	....
plant (n.)	....
arrange (*a meeting*) (v.)	....
cancel (*a meeting*) (v.)	....
change (*a meeting*) (v.)	....
confirm (*a meeting*) (v.)	....
increase (*sales*) (v.)	....
install (*equipment*) (v.)	....
introduce (*a new product*) (v.)	....
invest in (*equipment*) (v.)	....

UNIT 17 The Business Pleasure Trip

17.1

1 Vocabulary

Look at the words in the box and put them into groups like this:

Transport	Entertainment	Scenery
cab........	movie.........	mountain.....
....	....	....
....	....	....
....	....	....

> mountain cab movie
> show park lake
> subway car concert
> beach play bus
> coast jazz tram

2 Reading

Ms Hagihari is going on a business trip to Washington DC. It is her first visit to the States. Read this article and then answer her questions.

Metro: subway

1 I'd like to go to a classical concert. Where should I go?
You should go to:
a) the Smithsonian.
b) the Kennedy Center.
c) Capitol Hill.

2 I'd like to go out for an unusual meal. What can you recommend?
Why don't you try:
a) McDonalds?
b) the Everest Room in the Loop?
c) an Ethiopian restaurant?

3 Where can I buy a present for my children?
a) Fifth Avenue.
b) One of the museums.
c) Sorry, I've no idea.

4 Do I need to hire a car?
Not really. The best way to get around in Washington is:
a) by subway.
b) on foot.
c) by cab.

5 I'm going out to dinner. What should I wear?
a) A dress.
b) Your jeans.
c) Your work clothes.

WASHINGTON DC

Museums
This a museum town. Besides the National Gallery, the Corocoran and the Smithsonian, there are many smaller museums like the Phillips Collection, which has Impressionist and post-Impressionist masterpieces.

Concerts
Check the schedule at the Kennedy Center, where the National Symphony and the Washington Opera perform; also find out what's at the Arena Stage for new works, foreign productions and revivals. The best jazz and blues clubs are around Dupont Circle, and Capitol Hill.

Restaurants
Washington offers a range of ethnic eateries. Perhaps the most exotic cuisine is Ethiopian. Try the food at Fasikas or Meskerem in the Adams Morgan Section.

Sightseeing
Take a 20-minute drive to Old Town Alexandria and see the handsome 200-year-old brick houses. The Lee Fendall House (1785) and the Lloyd House Library (1797) are worth visiting.

Shopping
For interesting gifts under $25, few places are better than Washington. Every museum has a shop packed with reasonably priced reproductions, unusual books, old fashioned and high-tech children's games — even handicrafts and clothing.

Transport
A car is optional. The Metro, which closes at midnight, is convenient and clean.

Clothing
Wardrobe note: Washington is the most formal city in the country; you'll want a silk dress or a dinner suit for any evening activity above going for a drink.

60

17.2

1 Listening and speaking

Practise offering to do things.
Listen and repeat the offers like this:

Voice: Would you like me to book a hotel?
You: *(Beep)* Would you like me to book a hotel?

2 Reading

Look at these advertisements and find the following:

1 Classical music ....
2 Art exhibitions ....
3 Sport ....
4 Opera ....
5 Restaurants ....
6 Theatres ....

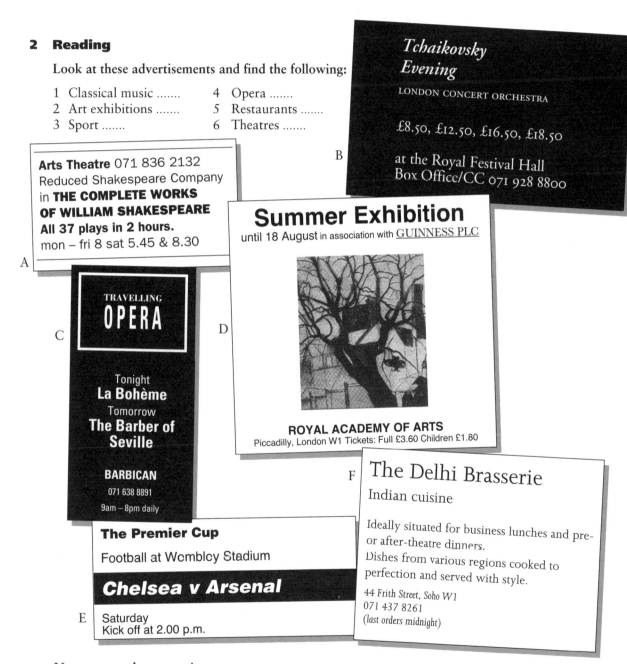

A
Arts Theatre 071 836 2132
Reduced Shakespeare Company
in **THE COMPLETE WORKS OF WILLIAM SHAKESPEARE**
All 37 plays in 2 hours.
mon – fri 8 sat 5.45 & 8.30

B
Tchaikovsky Evening
LONDON CONCERT ORCHESTRA
£8.50, £12.50, £16.50, £18.50
at the Royal Festival Hall
Box Office/CC 071 928 8800

C
TRAVELLING OPERA
Tonight **La Bohème**
Tomorrow **The Barber of Seville**
BARBICAN
071 638 8891
9am – 8pm daily

D
Summer Exhibition
until 18 August in association with GUINNESS PLC
ROYAL ACADEMY OF ARTS
Piccadilly, London W1 Tickets: Full £3.60 Children £1.80

E
The Premier Cup
Football at Wembley Stadium
Chelsea v Arsenal
Saturday
Kick off at 2.00 p.m.

F
The Delhi Brasserie
Indian cuisine
Ideally situated for business lunches and pre- or after-theatre dinners.
Dishes from various regions cooked to perfection and served with style.
44 Frith Street, Soho W1
071 437 8261
(last orders midnight)

Now answer these questions:
1 How much are the cheapest tickets for the Tchaikovsky concert? ....
2 What is the latest time you can order a meal? ....
3 What's on at the Barbican tomorrow? ....
4 What's the telephone number of the Arts Theatre? ....
5 When does the Summer Exhibition finish? ....
6 What time does the football match start on Saturday? ....

17.3

1 Language in use

Look at the pictures and write what the people say.

1 A: ....
  B: Is that the time?

2 A: ....
  B: Yes, that would be nice.

3 A: ....
  B: I'm glad you enjoyed it.

4 A: ....
  B: Thank you. I will.

2 Listening and speaking

Listen to Ritva Forslund talking to a colleague about a recent trip to Milan. Write true [T] or false [F] for each sentence.

1 She visited the new factory. [ ]
2 She had dinner with Taffarello on Tuesday. [ ]
3 She went to the opera on Friday. [ ]
4 She likes opera. [ ]
5 She went to a football match at the weekend. [ ]
6 The company has got the contract. [ ]

3 Writing

Rewrite Ms Forslund's letter of thanks with correct punctuation and layout. Use a separate sheet of paper.

> vittorio nanini
> via san martino 32
> 201 46 milan
> italy
>
> 1 july 199-
>
> dear mr nanini i am writing to thank you for your hospitality while i was in milan i had a very enjoyable time and i think the negotiations were very good for both our companies thank you again and i look forward to seeing you in helsinki in august yours sincerely ritva forslund

Reference section

Useful words and expressions

	Your translation
art (n.)	....
concert (n.)	....
exhibition (n.)	....
sightseeing (n.)	....
shopping (n.)	....
theatre (n.)	....
by bus	....
by taxi (BE) / cab (AE)	....
on foot	....
by underground (BE) / subway (AE)	....
Are you interested in …?	....
Do you want me to find out about …?	....
Don't worry.	....
If it's no trouble.	....
It's all right.	....
Shall I pick you up?	....
Would you like me to …?	....
Give my regards to …	....
I'm glad you enjoyed it.	....
It was a pleasure.	....

UNIT 18 Problems, problems

18.1

1 Listening and speaking

You will hear someone talking about a problem. Offer to help by phoning the correct department like this:

Voice: We need some more envelopes.
You: (*Beep*) I'll phone the Purchasing Department.

Choose from the departments in the box.

| Accounts | Personnel |
| Purchasing | Service |

2 Grammar

Underline the correct form of the future in *italics*.

A
A: I'd like to speak to someone in Marketing.
B: *I'm putting / I'll put* you through to Mr North ... I'm afraid he's in a meeting. Can I give him a message?
A: Don't worry. *I'm trying / I'll try* again tomorrow.

B
A: Could you ask Ms Osterloh to phone me about our order?
B: *I'm giving / I'll give* her the message.

C
A: *Are you doing / Will you do* anything tomorrow?
B: Just a minute, *I'm checking / I'll check* my diary ... *I'm going / I'll go* to the new factory in the afternoon.

3 Reading

Read this article. These figures are missing; where do you think they belong?

A 100   C £84,000   E C$500 million
B 72 billion   D 15 million miles F 300 billion

Clear your desk!

Visit the office of the head of any large company and you will find a tidy desk. Success, it seems, comes from learning how to control your paperwork.

But many of us try to work under a mountain of reports, memos, unanswered letters, trade magazines and brochures. 'Paperwork problems are at the centre of time management problems' says Declan Treacy, the author of a book called *Clear Your Desk*. Horrifying statistics prove this: office workers around the world use more than .... (1) of paper every year; there are .... (2) pieces of paper in American files; another .... (3) pages are added every year; Canadian businessmen spend more than .... (4) on paper storage; .... (5) office workers looking for bits of paper cost a British company .... (6) a year.

The essential rule is this: when paper arrives, deal with it once and once only. There are just four things you can do with it: throw it away (at least 30% of incoming mail is probably junk); file it (make sure you really need to keep it); pass it on to the person who is in a position to deal with it; or act on it.

18.2

1 Listening

Listen to this recorded phone call and complete the message.

Phone message

From: ....
Of: ....
Phone: ....

Message: ....
....
....
....

2 Language in use

Read this conversation and complete with with suitable words.

Gonzales: Sales department. Pedro Gonzales speaking.

Schutt: This is Gerda Schutt from Meiers. I'm .... (1) about our order for computer disks. There .... (2) to be a .... (3). We .... (4) article number 495 and you .... (5) us article number 594.

Gonzales: Just a moment. Could I have the .... (6) number?

Schutt: Let's see . . . It's DD 303.

Gonzales: Hold the .... (7) please, I'll just .... (8) it. ... I'm very .... (9), but we've had some .... (10) in the dispatch department. Could you return the disks? Of course we'll .... (11) the costs.

Schutt: Fine, but when can we expect .... (12) of the correct disks?

Gonzales: I'll make sure you get them by the end of the week.

3 Vocabulary

Complete this letter with words from the box.

| apologize | customers | manufacturers | orders | problems | products |

---

16 August 199-

Dear Customer

Enclosed is our latest price list, which is valid until the end of the year.

We have had some .... (1) with the Gizmo range of .... (2) over the last few months, and we .... (3) for this. We have contacted the .... (4) and they have informed us that they will meet all our future .... (5) promptly. We will monitor this very carefully as we wish to give our .... (6) the best service possible.

Yours sincerely

18.3

1 Vocabulary

Complete these sentences. Then write the missing words in the puzzle below and find the hidden word.

1 I'm afraid we have to .... our order.
2 We .... for the delay.
3 When we unpacked the machine, we noticed some .... to the casing.
4 We will .... any faulty goods free of charge.
5 There's a .... on orders.
6 The fax has broken down. We must .... it.
7 There seems to be a .... in the invoice.
8 We will .... your money if the goods are not satisfactory.

Hidden word ▼

	1	C	A	N	C	E	L	
2								
3								
4								
5								
6								
	7							
8								

Now complete this sentence with the hidden word:

You should .... if you have a problem!

2 Reading

Read this letter from Pacific Machines to Avalon Industries. What has Pacific Machines decided to do about the damaged machine? Tick the correct answer.

Refund the money. [ ]
Replace the machine. [ ]
Ask the customer to return the machine. [ ]
Refuse to accept responsibility. [ ]
None of the above. [ ]

Pacific Machines
212 Twin Dolphin Drive
Redwood City CA 94065
USA

Mr Rogers
Production Manager
Avalon Industries
28 Devonport Rd
Stoke
Plymouth PL3 4DW
England

August 10 199-

Dear Mr Rogers

Thank you for your letter of July 29 regarding order no. AS 671.
In your letter you state that the case was damaged and that the machine did not function when you turned it on. You also mention the possibility of the machine not being properly packed or tested before dispatch. I can assure you that the packing was our normal packing with which we have had no problems for over four years and I can guarantee you that the machine was tested before dispatch and that it was functioning.
The matter has been complicated as we received a fax on July 24 from your company stating that the machine had arrived in good condition.
As you are a valued client of ours we will do our best to solve the problem. My suggestion is for a technician from Electroservice, which has the service contract in England for our machines, to come to your company and inspect the machine and possibly fix it. Once we have his report we can then decide on what further action to take.
I hope this is satisfactory for you and I look forward to hearing from you soon.

Yours truly
Bob Olsen
Bob Olsen

3 Writing

You are Mr Rogers. Use these notes to write a letter in reply to Pacific Machines, with correct punctuation and layout. Use a separate sheet of paper.

> Fax sent on 24 July was a mistake
>
> Send technician as soon as possible
>
> If machine can't be repaired we need a replacement

Reference section

'Will' future

Positive

I You She He It We They	'll will	go. fly.

Negative

I You She He It We They	won't will not	go. fly.

Question

Will	I you she he it we they	go? fly?

Short answer

Yes,	I you she he it we they	will.	No,	I you she he it we they	won't. will not.

We use the 'will' future when we decide something at the moment of speaking:

> We need some more brochures.
> I'll **phone** Sales.
>
> Are you free on Monday?
> I'll just **check** my diary.

Remember: We use the present progressive to talk about future appointments and arrangements (see Unit 8):

> What **are** you **doing** on Monday?
> I'm **attending** a conference.

Useful words and expressions

	Your translation
apologize (v.)	....
break down (v.)	....
check (v.)	....
file (v.)	....
replace (*goods*) (v.)	....
refund (*money*) (v.)	....
Let's see.	....
I'll look into it.	....
I'll see what I can do.	....
There seems to be a mistake.	....

UNIT 19 Future trends

19.1

1 Vocabulary

Up or down? Write [↑] or [↓].

1 decline   [ ]   3 fall   [ ]   5 go up   [ ]
2 increase [ ]   4 decrease   [ ]   6 rise   [ ]

2 Language in use

These graphs show forecasts for next year. Look at them and write some sentences to describe what will happen. Use the words in the box to help you.

| rapidly | dramatically | slowly | slightly | steadily |

1 .Production will increase dramatically...........................
2 ....
3 ....
4 ....
5 ....
6 ....

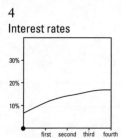

1 Production
2 Unemployment
3 Wages
4 Interest rates
5 Inflation
6 House prices

3 Reading

Read this article about the future of the airline industry and mark [↑] or [↓] for each item.

Flight to the unknown

The world's airline industry will change more quickly in the next twelve months than in any year since aviation began. Watch out for the following trends:

* Passenger traffic will go up by 4% a year in Europe. Asia will see even faster growth – up to 9% a year.

* Flight delays will become a nightmare. For travel under 700 km, high speed trains will be the answer. Paris to Lyon by train takes two hours; by plane it can take up to three – city centre to city centre.

* Air fares will not fall. Last year, airlines lost money so they will have to increase prices – or go bankrupt.

* There will be more competition. More small airlines will start up. Good. But as the number of flights increases, so will the congestion in the airports. So governments will need to spend more money on them. Otherwise there will be even more delays.

1 Number of passengers in Europe   [ ]
2 Number of passengers in Asia   [ ]
3 Delays   [ ]
4 Air fares   [ ]
5 Competition   [ ]
6 Number of new airlines   [ ]

19.2

1 Language in use

Read these sentences: how sure are people that things will happen? Write the numbers of the sentences in the correct box.

1 I'm certain the cost of living'll rise.
2 I don't think people'll want to work for big companies.
3 I'm sure robots won't replace factory workers.
4 I'm sure people'll want to learn foreign languages.
5 It's possible that the yen'll be more important than the dollar.
6 I expect people'll spend more money on holidays.
7 I'm certain people won't eat out so often.
8 I expect most people'll shop with credit cards.
9 It's possible that people'll work until they are seventy.
10 I don't expect computers'll become more user friendly.

100%	75%	50%	25%	0%
1,				7,

2 Listening and speaking

Here are two people's predictions for the next century.

Typical evening's entertainment	in a bar or café	at home with friends
Luxury items	time	travel
Average working week	longer	shorter

Now listen to different people's opinions about these predictions, and repeat like this:

Voice: I don't think people will spend their evenings in bars or cafés.
You: *(Beep)* I don't think people will spend their evenings in bars or cafés.

3 Writing

Complete these sentences with your own opinions.

.... people will spend their evenings in bars or cafés.
.... people will spend their evenings at home.
.... time will be a luxury item.
.... travel will be a luxury item.
.... the average working week will be longer.
.... the average working week will be shorter.

19.3

1 Reading

Read this article. Then answer the questions.

> # Telecommuter portrait:
>
> ## editing facts by fax
>
> Jennifer Porter is the managing editor of *Healthcare*, a publication of the American Pharmaceutical Association. From her private office in her Virginia home, she assigns up to ten articles for each issue of the magazine. The writers send her their stories on a computer disk, usually by means of an overnight delivery service. Porter checks them and then sends them to the designer's office in New York.
>
> Porter's biggest problem with electronic publishing is training her writers. 'One sent the story on a wrong-sized disk; another used a disk that my computer couldn't read; a third used software I couldn't decipher.'
>
> The disk problems should improve on the next issue because Porter has recently invested in a modem so that writers can send their stories directly to her computer.
>
> Porter says she is a skeptical technical consumer. 'I like a computer the same way I like a pencil. They are both tools that must work. If something goes wrong with my electronic equipment out here in the middle of Virginia, I have to put it in the car and take it someplace.'

1 Tick [✓] the equipment which is mentioned in the article:
   [ ] computer   [ ] telex
   [ ] photocopier [ ] modem
   [ ] portable phone [ ] fax

2 Are these statements true [T] or false [F]?
   A Jennifer Porter is a writer for a medical magazine. [ ]
   B Her biggest problem is her computer. [ ]
   C She recently bought a modem. [ ]
   D She is a hi-tech fan. [ ]

2 Listening

Listen to this man talking about telecommuting. Write true [T] or false [F] for each sentence.

1 He started telecommuting last year. [ ]
2 In London he worked two or three hours a day. [ ]
3 Now he works ten hours a day. [ ]
4 He is the company's only employee. [ ]
5 His secretary now lives in Ireland. [ ]
6 She earns more now than she did before. [ ]

Reference section

'Will' future for predictions

We use the 'will' future to talk about things we think will or won't happen in the future.

> The dollar **will fall** next year.
> Food prices **will rise** by 4% next year.
> Wages **will increase** by 10% next year.

If you say that something will not happen then you use the contracted form **won't**.

> Housing costs **won't** increase next year.

Remember: We also use the 'will' future when we decide something at the moment of speaking (see Unit 18).

Useful words and expressions

	Your translation
forecast (n.)	....
housing (n.)	....
inflation (n.)	....
interest rates (n.)	....
production (n.)	....
unemployment (n.)	....
wages (n.)	....
decrease (v.)	....
fall (v.)	....
go down (v.)	....
go up (v.)	....
rise (v.)	....
dramatically (adv.)	....
rapidly (adv.)	....
slightly (adv.)	....
slowly (adv.)	....
I'm certain ...	....
I expect ...	....
It's possible ...	....
I'm sure ...	....
I think ...	....

UNIT 20 Progress test 4

20.1 Grammar

Fill in the correct past simple form of the verb in (brackets).

Five years ago production at Greville Motors .... (*rise*) (1) to 53,000 cars a year. Then the dollar .... (*fall*) (2). Prices in America .... (*go*) (3) up and sales .... (*decline*) (4) dramatically. Greville then .... (*try*) (5) to increase sales at home and in other markets, especially Japan. It also .... (*stop*) (6) production of its cheapest model, the 670, and .... (*start*) (7) selling more expensive cars. For a short time this .... (*be*) (8) very successful.

Now fill in the correct form of the present perfect.

This year .... (*not be*) (9) a good year for Greville. Sales .... (*begin*) (10) to fall again. Profits .... (*fall*) (11) to $30 million and the company .... (*cut*) (12) the number of employees to 8,600.

20.2 Grammar

Write short answers to these questions:

1 Have you read the sales report?
  Yes, ...
2 Did sales go up last year?
  No, ...
3 Will they go up next year?
  Yes, ...
4 Did exports to the USA increase last year?
  Yes, ...
5 Will they increase again next year?
  No, ...
6 Has your boss seen the report too?
  No, ...

20.3 Grammar

Complete these sentences with a suitable word.

1 Sales have risen .... 10%.
2 Production has increased .... 2,000 units to 2,500 units.
3 Sales usually increase .... Christmas time.
4 I'm sure there will be a fall .... interest rates.
5 Unemployment always increases .... winter.
6 I think there will be a rise .... 15% in production.

20.4 Language in use

Write a suitable response to each sentence.

1 Thanks for arranging that.   ....
2 The printer isn't working.   ....
3 Would you like me to call a taxi?   ....
4 We need a new price list.   ....
5 Would you like to see anything else? ....
6 Give my regards to Maria.   ....

20.5 Vocabulary

Look at the words in the box and put them into groups. Then add some more.

| rise | investments | exhibition | unemployment | museum | production | theatre |
| increase | sales | decline | wages | fall | restaurant | equipment | inflation |

Entertainment	Trends	Business information	Company report
..exhibition.........	rise....................	unemployment....	investments.......
....	....	....	....
....	....	....	....
....	....	....	....
....	....	....	....

20.6 Listening

Look at the graph comparing the price of an average bag of potato chips in different countries in South East Asia. Some prices in the graph are wrong. Listen to the tape and correct them.

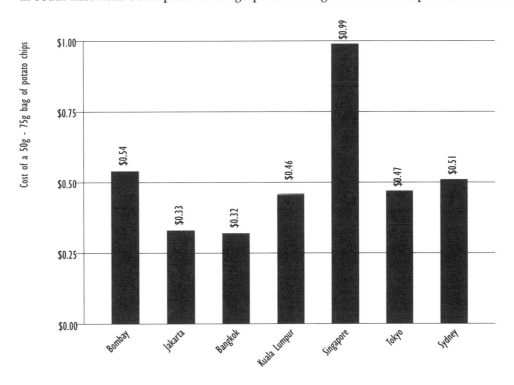

Key and tapescripts

Unit 1

1.1

1 2 Good evening 3 Good afternoon
4 Good morning

2 2 's 3 Are 4 am 5 is 6 isn't 7 's 8 Are
9 'm not 10 'm 11 Is 12 it is 13 Are 14 are

3 2 A 3 C 4 B

1.2

Hidden word ▼

```
      1 B R A Z I L
      2 R U S S I A
      3 A U S T R A L I A
J A P A N
F R A N C E
      6 C H I N A
      7 E G Y P T
   8  S P A I N
```

1

2 2 C 3 E 4 B 5 F 6 D

🔊 Listen and check your answers.

A
Man: Hello, Mr Svenson. It's good to see you again. How are you?
Svenson: Fine, thanks. And how are you?

B
Chung: Excuse me, are you Ms Pilarski?
Pilarski: Yes, I am.
Chung: My name's Tina Chung. I work in our Taipei branch. How do you do?
Pilarski: How do you do?

3 🔊 Practise introductions and greetings.
First, listen and repeat like this:

Voice: Pleased to meet you.
You: (Beep) Pleased to meet you.
Voice: Pleased to meet you.

Now you try.

1 V: Pleased to meet you.
       (Beep and pause for repeat)
   V: Pleased to meet you.

2 V: How do you do?
       (Beep and pause for repeat)
   V: How do you do?

3 V: How are you?
       (Beep and pause for repeat)
   V: How are you?

4 V: Nice to see you again.
       (Beep and pause for repeat)
   V: Nice to see you again.

Now listen and answer like this:

Voice 1: Pleased to meet you.
You: (Beep) Pleased to meet you, too.
Voice 2: Pleased to meet you, too.
You: (Beep) Pleased to meet you, too.
Voice 2: Pleased to meet you, too.

Now you try.

1 V1: Pleased to meet you.
        (Beep and pause for response)
   V2: Pleased to meet you, too.
        (Beep and pause to repeat)
   V2: Pleased to meet you, too.

2 V1: How do you do?
        (Beep and pause for response)
   V2: How do you do?
        (Beep and pause to repeat)
   V2: How do you do?

3 V1: How are you?
        (Beep and pause for response)
   V2: Fine, thanks.
        (Beep and pause to repeat)
   V2: Fine, thanks.

4 V1: Nice to see you again.
        (Beep and pause for response)
   V2: Nice to see you again, too.
        (Beep and pause to repeat)
   V2: Nice to see you again, too.

1.3

1 *Possible answers*
2 I'd like to introduce Mr Kim. He's from Korea. He works in Seoul.
3 This is Ms Rao. She's from India. She works in Bombay.
4 I'd like to introduce Mrs Manos. She's from Greece. She works in Athens.
5 This is Mr Regueira. He's from Brazil. He works in São Paulo.
6 I'd like to introduce Ms Ersoy. She's from Turkey. She works in Istanbul.

2 1 nice/good   2 are   3 introduce   4 meet
5 about   6 sugar   7 this   8 do   9 call   10 is

3 1 January   2 March   3 April   4 May   5 August
6 September   7 October   8 December
A Monday   B Tuesday   C Thursday   D Friday
E Saturday   F Sunday

Unit 2

2.1

1 1 an   2 a   3 a   4 an   5 a   6 a   7 an   8 an

2 2 He's a bank manager.
3 They're engineers.
4 She's an accountant.
5 They're sales clerks.
6 She's a lawyer.

Listen and underline the number you hear.
3 1 12%   2 2%   3 30%   4 8%   5 15%   6 66%

2.2

1 2F   3E   4D   5C   6B

2 255 Sussex Street, Sydney, NSW 2000

Listen and complete the address:

... and our address is Horner and Horner, that's H.O.R.N.E.R, 255 Sussex Street, that's S.U.S.S.E.X, Sydney, that's S.Y.D.N.E.Y, New South Wales. If you just write NSW, that's OK. Er ... NSW 2000.

3 1 Good   2 like   3 to   4 speaking   5 from
6 Hold   7 This   8 Sorry   9 your   10 speak
11 moment   12 Thank you

2.3

1 Practice asking questions about people. First, listen and repeat like this:

Voice: What's his surname?
You: (*Beep*) What's his surname?
Voice: What's his surname?

Now you try.

1 V: What's his surname?
       (*Beep and pause to repeat*)
    V: What's his surname?

2 V: Can you spell that, please?
       (*Beep and pause to repeat*)
    V: Can you spell that, please?

3 V: What does he do?
       (*Beep and pause to repeat*)
    V: What does he do?

4 V: Who does he work for?
       (*Beep and pause to repeat*)
    V: Who does he work for?

5 V: What's his telephone number?
       (*Beep and pause to repeat*)
    V: What's his telephone number?

6 V: Can you repeat that, please?
       (*Beep and pause to repeat*)
    V: Can you repeat that, please?

Now listen and answer like this:

Voice 1: What's his surname?
You: (*Beep*) His surname's Sirotto.
Voice 2: His surname's Sirotto.
You: (*Beep*) His surname's Sirotto.
Voice 2: His surname's Sirotto.

Now you try.

1 V1: What's his surname?
        (*Beep and pause for response*)
    V2: His surname's Sirotto.
        (*Beep and pause to repeat*)
    V2: His surname's Sirotto.

2 V1: Could you spell that, please?
        (*Beep and pause for response*)
    V2: S.I.R.O.T.T.O.
        (*Beep and pause to repeat*)
    V2: S.I.R.O.T.T.O.

3 V1: What does he do?
        (*Beep and pause for response*)
    V2: He's a product manager.
        (*Beep and pause to repeat*)
    V2: He's a product manager.

4 V1: Who does he work for?
        (*Beep and pause for response*)

V2: He works for Gizmo Gadgets Ltd.
(Beep and pause to repeat)
V2: He works for Gizmo Gadgets Ltd.

5 V1: What's his telephone number?
(Beep and pause for response)
V2: It's 0793 626315.
(Beep and pause to repeat)
V2: It's 0793 626315.

6 V1: Can you repeat that, please?
(Beep and pause for response)
V2: It's 0793 626315.
(Beep and pause to repeat)
V2: It's 0793 626315.

2 2 What's her surname?
3 Who does she work for?
4 What's her/the address?
5 What's her telephone number?
6 What's her fax number?

Debra Hartmann
Accountant

AMB Inc.

23 Wheeler Street
Boston, Mass
Tel: 497 3421
Fax: 491 4362

Listen and fill in the woman's business card.

Man: Can I have that accountant's name, please?
Woman: Yes, it's Hartmann. Debra Hartmann.
Man: Is that Hartmann with one n or two?
Woman: Two – H.A.R.T.M.A.N.N.
Man: Right. And what's her first name again?
Woman: Debra – that's D.E.B.R.A.
Man: And who does she work for?
Woman: AMB Inc.
Man: AMB? Oh yes. I know them. OK, I'll send it there. Now, what's the address?
Woman: Uh … 23 Wheeler Street, Boston, Mass.
Man: 23 Wheeler Street, Boston, Mass.
Woman: Do you want her phone number too?
Man: Er … yes, please.
Woman: It's 497 3421.
Man: I'm sorry, that was too quick. Can you repeat that?
Woman: Yes, it's 497 –
Man: 497 –
Woman: 3421.
Man: 3421. Thanks. Do you have her fax number?
Woman: Um … hold on … uh, 491 4362.
Man: 491 4362. That's great. Thanks a lot for your help.

Unit 3

3.1

1 2 German 3 Dutch 4 Swedish 5 Japanese 6 American

2 1 C 2 D 3 B 4 A

Listen and give the correct headquarters like this:

Voice 1: The headquarters of Coca Cola are in New York.
You: *(Beep)* No, they're not. They're in Atlanta.
Voice 2: No, they're not. They're in Atlanta.
You: *(Beep)* No, they're not. They're in Atlanta.
Voice 2: No, they're not. They're in Atlanta.

Now you try.
1 V1: The headquarters of Coca Cola are in New York.
(Beep and pause for response)
V2: No, they're not. They're in Atlanta.
(Beep and pause to repeat)
V2: No, they're not. They're in Atlanta.

2 V1: The headquarters of Bayer are in Munich.
(Beep and pause for response)
V2: No, they're not. They're in Leverkusen.
(Beep and pause to repeat)
V2: No, they're not. They're in Leverkusen.

3 V1: The headquarters of Olivetti are in Milan.
(Beep and pause for response)
V2: No, they're not. They're in Ivrea.
(Beep and pause to repeat)
V2: No, they're not. They're in Ivrea.

4 V1: The headquarters of Aeroflot are in Kiev.
(Beep and pause for response)
V2: No, they're not. They're in Moscow.
(Beep and pause to repeat)
V2: No, they're not. They're in Moscow.

3 1 I work for Higgins Electronics.
2 We're a British company.
3 Our headquarters are in Glasgow.
4 We have branches in New York, London and Frankfurt.
5 One of our competitors is Total Electronics.
6 They're a Taiwanese company.
7 Their headquarters are in Taipei.
8 They have branches in San Francisco, London and Tokyo.

3.2

1 3 S 4 M 5 M 6 M 7 S 8 M 9 S

3 1 Is 2 does 3 Do 4 Are 5 do 6 Does
1 B 2 D 3 F 4 E 6 C

3.3

1 2 F 3 D 4 A 5 B 6 E

2 1 What's your turnover?
2 How many people do you employ?
3 What are your main businesses?
4 How many subsidiaries do you have?
5 Where are your subsidiaries?

1 $12,850 million 2 13,426 3 oil, chemicals
4 30 5 USA, Asia

🔊 Listen to someone talking about AFL and fill in the missing information.

Woman: Can you tell me something about AFL? For example, what's your annual turnover?
Man: Let me see, last year it was US$12,850 million.
Woman: 12,850 million dollars. That's quite a lot of money! So, how many people do you employ?
Man: At the moment we have 13,426 on the payroll.
Woman: 13,426. You're a big company! Now, I know you do all sorts of things, but what are your main businesses?
Man: Our main businesses ... oils and chemicals.
Woman: And ... er ... how many subsidiaries do you have?
Man: 30 altogether.
Woman: 30. Where are your subsidiaries?
Man: Mainly in the United States and then there's also a few in Asia...

Unit 4

4.1

1 2 After-sales is on the second floor.
3 The canteen is on the third floor.
4 Sales is on the first floor.
5 Accounts is on the fifth floor.
6 Production is on the ground floor.
7 Personnel is on the sixth floor.
8 Research and Development is on the fourth floor.
9 The M.D's office is on the seventh/top floor.

2 1 second 2 right 3 between 4 Go 5 floor
6 turn 7 fourth 8 left 9 next to

4.2

1 Hidden word ▼

1 DEVELOPS
2 EMPLOYEES
3 PAYMENT
4 ADVERTISES
5 MARKETS
6 STOCK
7 MAKES
8 SELLS
9 SENDS
10 CUSTOMERS

2 1 cheque 2 price list 3 c.v. 4 invoice
5 order form 6 catalogue

3 1 catalogue 2 price list 3 order form

4.3

1 1 Could/Can 2 through 3 Department 4 in
5 take 6 her 7 course 8 calling/speaking
9 connect 10 with 11 Can 12 message 13 ask
14 me 15 Certainly 16 Who's

2 1 C 2 D 3 B 4 A

🔊 Listen and ask for the correct department like this:

Voice: I'm calling about my order number 384.
You: (Beep) Could you put me through to the Sales Department?
Voice: Could you put me through to the Sales Department?
You: (Beep) Could you put me through to the Sales Department?
Voice: Could you put me through to the Sales Department?

Now you try.

1 V: I'm, calling about my order number 384.
   (Beep and pause for response)
   V: Could you put me through to the Sales Department?
   (Beep and pause to repeat)
   V: Could you put me through to the Sales Department?

2 V: I'd like to speak to someone about an invoice.
   (Beep and pause for response)
   V: Could you put me through to the Accounts Department?
   (Beep and pause to repeat)
   V: Could you put me through to the Accounts Department?

3 V: I've got a problem with the copier I bought last month.
   (Beep and pause for response)
   V: Could you put me through to the After-sales Department?
   (Beep and pause to repeat)
   V: Could you put me through to the After-sales Department?

4 V: I'm calling about your advertisement for a Sales Clerk.
   (*Beep and pause for response*)
   V: Could you connect me with the Personnel Department?
   (*Beep and pause to repeat*)
   V: Could you connect me with the Personnel Department?

3

```
              Phone Message

    For:      Nigel Fielding

    From:     Gerda Lange

    Of:       NFC

    Phone:    244 344

    Message:  Please call her back
```

Listen to this phone call and fill in the phone message form.

Recept: Beris Foods. Good afternoon.
Lange: Er ... this is Gerda Lange from NFC. I'd like to speak to Nigel Fielding.
Recept: Hold the line, please. I'll put you through.
Cope: Nick Cope. Good afternoon.
Lange: Oh ... good afternoon. My name's Gerda Lange. I'm from NFC. I'd like to speak to Nigel Fielding.
Cope: I'm afraid he's in a meeting. Er, can I help you?
Lange: Oh, I see. Er, yes. Can you ask him to call me back? My name's Lange. That's L.A.N.G.E, and I'm from NFC.
Cope: Gerda Lange from NFC.... Er, of course. Er ... has he got your number?
Lange: I think so. But anyway, it's 244 344.
Cope: 244 344. Right, Ms Lange. I'll ask him to call you as soon as he gets back.
Lange: Thank you very much.
Cope: You're welcome.

Unit 5

5.1 2 's / is   3 'm / am   4 works   5 work   6 is
7 are   8 have   9 is   10 produces   11 are
12 exports

5.2 2 Yes, it does   3 No, it isn't   4 Yes, we do
5 No, we don't   6 Yes, of course / Yes, it does

5.3 1 on   2 for / at   3 on   4 at / in   5 at   6 on

5.4 *Possible answers*
1 Pleased to meet you.
2 How are you?
3 What do you do?
4 How about some coffee?
5 Excuse me, I'm looking for Mr Tan's office / where's Mr Tan's office?
6 Thank you.

5.5 1 France (the others are nationalities)
2 branch (the others are jobs)
3 Accountant (the others are departments)
4 ten (the others are ordinal numbers)
5 headquarters (the others are types of business)
6 February (the others are days of the week)

5.6 *Possible answers*
1 Good morning, this is (*name*) speaking.
2 I'm sorry, who's speaking/calling?
3 I'm afraid he's on vacation this week.
4 She's in a meeting. Can I take a message?
5 Of course. What's your telephone number?
6 Right. Thank you. Goodbye.

5.7 1 correct   2 correct   3 15 computers
4 It's urgent

Read this telephone message. Then listen to the phone call and check if the numbered information in the message is correct. Write any corrections to the message below.

Recept: Good morning. Reed Electronics. Can I help you?
Taylor: This is Mark Taylor from DataSystems here. Could you put me through to Mr Salomon?
Recept: Hold the line, please.
Woman: Sales Department.
Taylor: Ah, good morning. This is Mark Taylor from DataSystems here. Is Mr Salomon there?
Woman: I'm afraid he's in a meeting.
Taylor: I see. Er ... can you give him a message?
Woman: Yes, of course.
Taylor: Can you ask him to phone Mark Taylor, that's T.A.Y.L.O.R, from DataSystems? It's about my order for fifteen computers. It's urgent, so can you ask him to phone me back today?
Woman: OK. Can I have your telephone number, too?
Taylor: Yes, it's 0648 49684.
Woman: 0648 49684. Right, Mr Taylor, I'll give Mr Salomon the message as soon as he gets back.

Unit 6

6.1

1 1 F 2 F 3 T 4 T 5 T 6 F

> Listen to Ana Campos talking about her working times and write true [T] or false [F].

Inter: Ana, can you tell me something about the working hours in your company?
Ana: Well, we have flexitime. I have to be in the office by half past eight and I can leave any time after three thirty. Um ... I'm not really a morning person, so I'm lucky if I get in on time. I usually start work around eight thirty and then leave the office some time between five and six.
Inter: And when do you go to lunch?
Ana: Well, the lunch break is between twelve and two. But I hardly ever have time for breakfast before I go to work, so I get very hungry. I usually try to go to lunch at twelve o'clock.
Inter: And how long do you have for lunch?
Ana: Three quarters of an hour.
Inter: How long is your working week?
Ana: Hmm, 40 hours, unfortunately. But I always work more hours from Monday to Thursday so I can take Friday afternoon off.

2 *at:* 12.30, lunchtime, noon.
on: 1 May, Friday, Tuesday morning.
in: the morning, summer, 1997.

1 at; at   2 on   3 in   4 on

3 1 Japan   2 Sweden   3 Holland   4 Sweden
5 Holland   6 Japan

6.2

1 2 do; start   3 do; have   4 do; have   5 does; leave
6 do; do
1 B   2 E   3 D   5 F   6 C

2 A friend phones you to tell you about their new job. Unfortunately the line is bad and you can't understand everything. Listen and ask questions like this:

Voice 1: I go to work by ...
You: (Beep) I'm sorry, how do you get to work?
Voice 2: I'm sorry, how do you get to work?
You: (Beep) I'm sorry, how do you get to work?
Voice 2: I'm sorry, how do you get to work?

Now you try.

1 V1: I go to work by ...
   (Beep and pause for response)
   V2: I'm sorry, how do you get to work?
   (Beep and pause to repeat)
   V2: I'm sorry, how do you get to work?

2 V1: I start work at ... thirty.
   (Beep and pause for response)
   V2: I'm sorry, when do you start work?
   (Beep and pause to repeat)
   V2: I'm sorry, when do you start work?

3 V1: I go to lunch at ...
   (Beep and pause for response)
   V2: I'm sorry, when do you go to lunch?
   (Beep and pause to repeat)
   V2: I'm sorry, when do you go to lunch?

4 V1: We have ... for lunch.
   (Beep and pause for response)
   V2: I'm sorry, how long do you have for lunch?
   (Beep and pause to repeat)
   V2: I'm sorry, how long do you have for lunch?

5 V1: I leave the office at quarter past ...
   (Beep and pause for response)
   V2: I'm sorry, when do you leave the office?
   (Beep and pause to repeat)
   V2: I'm sorry, when do you leave the office?

6 V1: I usually ... in the evening.
   (Beep and pause for response)
   V2: I'm sorry, what do you do in the evening?
   (Beep and pause to repeat)
   V2: I'm sorry, what do you do in the evening?

3 2 I hardly ever meet customers.
3 My boss goes on trips three times a year.
4 The Sales Department entertains visitors once a month.
5 I sometimes work late.
6 We often go to meetings.
7 Do you read the *Financial Times* every day?

6.3

1

	Salary	Hours	Holidays	Other benefits
A	£12,000	flexitime 35 hours	6 weeks	free lunches, bonus
B	£19,494	flexitime	24 days	

Hidden word ▼

1. C O L L E A G U E S
2. B O S S
3. C A N T E E N
4. H O L I D A Y
5. S H I F T
6. V A C A T I O N
7. I N T E R E S T I N G
8. H O U R S
9. J O U R N E Y
10. S A L A R Y

3 2 F 3 A 4 B 5 E 6 D
2 She doesn't mind working late.
3 She likes making phone calls.
4 She hates writing reports.
5 She doesn't like working with the computer.
6 She doesn't mind going to meetings.

Unit 7

7.1

1 1 makes 2 does 3 makes 4 makes 5 does
6 makes

2 *Possible answers*
2 Could you tell me the time, please?
3 Could/Would you make some coffee, please?
4 Could/Would you lend me some money, please?
5 Could/Would you copy this letter, please?
6 Could you work on Saturday, please?

3 🎧 Practise asking people to do things and answering them.
First, listen and repeat the requests like this:

Voice: Could you spell 'personnel', please?
You: (*Beep*) Could you spell 'personnel', please?
Voice: Could you spell 'personnel', please?

Now you try.
1 V: Could you spell 'personnel', please?
   (*Beep and pause to repeat*)
   V: Could you spell 'personnel', please?

2 V: Could you spell your surname, please?
   (*Beep and pause to repeat*)
   V: Could you spell your surname, please?

3 V: Could you give me your telephone number, please?
   (*Beep and pause to repeat*)
   V: Could you give me your telephone number, please?

4 V: Could you speak more slowly, please?
   (*Beep and pause to repeat*)
   V: Could you speak more slowly, please?

Now listen and answer like this:

Voice 1: Could you spell 'personnel', please?
You: (*Beep*) Sure. That's P.E.R.S.O.N.N.E.L.
Voice 2: Sure. That's P.E.R.S.O.N.N.E.L.

Now you try. There are no correct answers; use your own information to answer the requests!

1 V: Could you spell 'personnel', please?
   (*Beep and pause for response*)

2 V: Could you spell your surname, please?
   (*Beep and pause for response*)

3 V: Could you give me your telephone number, please?
   (*Beep and pause for response*)

4 V: Could you speak more slowly, please?
   (*Beep and pause for response*)

7.2

1 1 Y 2 Y 3 N 4 Y 5 N 6 Y

🎧 Listen to Armel Dubois talking about his new job. Then answer yes [Y] or no [N] to the questions.

Woman: So tell me something about your new job.
Armel: Well, the work's very interesting, but it's also very stressful.
Woman: Oh, really? Why's that?
Armel: Well, to begin with, I have to work very long hours. I have to be in the office at seven most days. And then I also have to travel a lot.
Woman: Do you? Do you have to go to conferences?
Armel: No, no. I have to, er, visit our customers, and they're all over the country so I'm hardly ever at home during the week.
Woman: Oh, I see. Do you have to use your own car?
Armel: Fortunately not. I've got a company car. That's one of the perks of the job. And the other good thing is that, er, I can take my holiday when I like. I don't have to take it in the summer any more.
Woman: Oh, that's good.
Armel: But I haven't told you the worst thing. I have to write a monthly report for my boss.
Woman: Well, so do I.
Armel: Yes, but it has to be in English!

2 2 needn't 3 mustn't 4 needn't 5 mustn't
6 mustn't

7.3

1 1 E 2 B 3 D 4 A 5 F 6 C

2 *Possible answers*
2 You shouldn't work so hard.
3 You should work near home.
4 Why don't you have English lessons?
5 You should learn to relax.
6 Why don't you ask him to stop?

Unit 8

8.1

1 2 He's having lunch with Ann on Tuesday.
3 He's meeting the production manager on Wednesday morning.
4 He's visiting the new factory on Wednesday afternoon.
5 He's finalizing the sales contract on Thursday morning.
6 He's going to the Computer Fair on Thursday afternoon.

2 2 F 3 A 4 E 5 B 6 C

8.2

1 2 Where are you staying?
3 Which companies are you visiting?
4 How long are you staying?
5 Who are you seeing?
6 When are you leaving?

2 You phone Mr Zuckermann's secretary about his visit to your company. It's a very bad line and you can't understand everything. Ask questions like this:

Secretary: He's arriving at ... o'clock.
You: (*Beep*) I'm sorry, when's he arriving?
Voice: I'm sorry, when's he arriving?
You: (*Beep*) I'm sorry, when's he arriving?
Voice: I'm sorry, when's he arriving?

Now you try.

1 S: He's arriving at ... o'clock.
    (*Beep and pause for response*)
  V: I'm sorry, when's he arriving?
    (*Beep and pause to repeat*)
  V: I'm sorry, when's he arriving?

2 S: He's staying at the ... Hotel.
    (*Beep and pause for response*)
  V: I'm sorry, which hotel is he staying at?
    (*Beep and pause to repeat*)
  V: I'm sorry, which hotel is he staying at?

3 S: He's staying for ... days.
    (*Beep and pause for response*)
  V: I'm sorry, how long is he staying?
    (*Beep and pause to repeat*)
  V: I'm sorry, how long is he staying?

4 S: He's seeing Mrs ... on Monday.
    (*Beep and pause for response*)
  V: I'm sorry, who's he seeing on Monday?
    (*Beep and pause to repeat*)
  V: I'm sorry, who's he seeing on Monday?

5 S: He's having dinner with Mrs Smith on ... evening.
    (*Beep and pause for response*)
  V: I'm sorry, when's he having dinner with Mrs Smith?
    (*Beep and pause to repeat*)
  V: I'm sorry, when's he having dinner with Mrs Smith?

6 S: He's flying to ... on Thursday.
    (*Beep and pause for response*)
  V: I'm sorry, where's he flying to on Thursday?
    (*Beep and pause to repeat*)
  V: I'm sorry, where's he flying to on Thursday?

3 1 that 2 speaking 3 How 4 fine 5 arrange/fix 6 free 7 afraid 8 what/how 9 about 10 on 11 suit 12 see

8.3

1 Hidden word ▼

1 STAYING
2 CATCHING
3 HAVING
4 MEETING
5 ATTENDING
6 LUNCH
7 FLYING
8 LEAVING

2

9 Monday	11 Wednesday
11.30 Planning meeting	10.30 Steve Morgan
2.00 Sales team	2.30 Mr Gardini
10 Tuesday	**12 Thursday**
10.30 Maria Rodriguez	11.00 Rich Calder
	13 Friday

2 A secretary is making appointments for her boss, Diana Dinkel. Listen to the phone calls and write the appointments in the diary.

A

Sec:	Diana Dinkel's office. Good morning.
Rodriguez:	Oh, good morning. My name's Maria Rodriguez from Servico. I'm coming to Chicago next week and I'd like to arrange a meeting with Ms Dinkel.
Sec:	I'm sorry, who's calling?
Rodriguez:	My name's Rodriguez, Maria Rodriguez from Servico.
Sec:	Oh yes, or course. Er, what day would suit you best, Ms Rodriguez?
Rodriguez:	Is Ms Dinkel free on Tuesday?
Sec:	I'll just check her diary … Yes, Tuesday's fine. Morning or afternoon?
Rodriguez:	Er … the morning. Is ten thirty OK?
Sec:	Yes, that's fine. Tuesday morning at ten thirty.
Rodriguez:	Great. Thank you very much. Goodbye.

B

Sec:	Diana Dinkel's office. Good morning.
Calder:	Hello Marita, it's Rich Calder speaking.
Sec:	Oh, hi Rich. How are you?
Calder:	Not too bad. And you?
Sec:	Fine, fine.
Calder:	Look, I need to see Diana about the new production plan. Is she free on Tuesday?
Sec:	Well, she's seeing a supplier in the morning, but she's not doing anything in the afternoon.
Calder:	Hm. I'm afraid the afternoon's no good. I've got a meeting with the engineers then. What about Thursday morning?
Sec:	Yes, in fact she's free all day Thursday at the moment. Er … what time?
Calder:	Eleven o'clock would be good.
Sec:	Right then, eleven o'clock on Thursday.
Calder:	Yes. Thanks a lot. Bye.

3

```
                              June 3, 199-

Dear Mr Gardini

I am writing to confirm your
appointment with Ms Dinkel on
Wednesday, June 11 at 2.30 in
Ms Dinkel's office.

Best regards

Marita Collins

Marita Collins
```

Unit 9

9.1

1 *Business:* conference, trade fair, meeting.
Travel: flight, trip.
Weather: wet, overcast, windy.

2 1 was 2 did 3 was 4 was 5 didn't 6 Were
7 weren't 8 was 9 Did 10 didn't

3 24% New Zealand; 23% Europe; 19% the Americas
13% business; 54% holidays

9.2

1 See 2 tapescript for answers
1 F 2 E 3 C 4 D 6 B

2 Listen and repeat the questions like this:

Voice: What was the conference like?
You: (Beep) What was the conference like?
Voice: What was the conference like?

Now you try.
1 V: What was the conference like?
   (Beep and pause to repeat)
   V: What was the conference like?

2 V: What was the hotel like?
   (Beep and pause to repeat)
   V: What was the hotel like?

3 V: What was the food like?
   (Beep and pause to repeat)
   V: What was the food like?

4 V: What were the speakers like?
   (Beep and pause to repeat)
   V: What were the speakers like?

5 V: What were the other people like?
   (Beep and pause to repeat)
   V: What were the other people like?

6 V: What was the weather like?
   (Beep and pause to repeat)
   V: What was the weather like?

3 See 4 tapescript for answers
1 B 3 D 4 E 5 F 6 C

4 Listen and repeat the questions like this:

Voice: Did you enjoy the conference?
You: (Beep) Did you enjoy the conference?
Voice: Did you enjoy the conference?

Now you try.
1 V: Did you enjoy the conference?

(*Beep and pause to repeat*)
V: Did you enjoy the conference?

2 V: Did you stay at the Hilton?
(*Beep and pause to repeat*)
V: Did you stay at the Hilton?

3 V: Did you meet Dr Yamamoto?
(*Beep and pause to repeat*)
V: Did you meet Dr Yamamoto?

4 V: Did you go to a lot of workshops?
(*Beep and pause to repeat*)
V: Did you go to a lot of workshops?

5 V: Did you learn anything?
(*Beep and pause to repeat*)
V: Did you learn anything?

6 V: Did you have a good time?
(*Beep and pause to repeat*)
V: Did you have a good time?

9.3

1 2 B 3 E 4 A 5 F 6 D

2 1 F 2 T 3 F 4 F 5 T 6 T

Listen to a guest registering at a hotel. Write true [T] or false [F] for each sentence.

Guest: Good evening. I need some accommodation for tonight.
Recept: Right, Madam. Just for one night?
Guest: Yes, that's right. Er … how much is a single room?
Recept: Eighty five pounds a night.
Guest: Does that include breakfast?
Recept: Yes, it does.
Guest: Right. Er … I have to leave early tomorrow morning. What time is breakfast?
Recept: From seven to ten.
Guest: Fine. Now, I have to make a phone call to Korea. Can I do that from my room?
Recept: Yes, of course. That's no problem.
Guest: And what about sending faxes? Is there somewhere I can send a fax from?
Recept: Yes, there are fax machines in the business centre. That's over there. Second door on the right.
Guest: Good. Now, because I'm leaving early tomorrow, is it all right if I pay now?
Recept: Oh, you can do it in the morning. It'll only take a minute, Madam.
Guest: Do you take American Express?
Recept: Yes, …

Unit 10

10.1 2 didn't come 3 was 4 'm going
5 's coming 6 're flying 7 'm staying
8 're going 9 're meeting 10 'm having
11 's not coming / isn't coming 12 's catching

10.2 2 My boss usually prepares the reports.
3 He rarely makes phone calls before nine o'clock.
4 I go on business trips twice a year.
5 Do you meet clients every day?
6 We normally go to the sales conference.

10.3 1 What do you do?
2 Who do you work for?
3 How do you get to work?
4 Where do you have lunch?
5 When do you finish work?
6 What do you do in the evening / at the weekend?

10.4 1 at 2 on 3 on 4 on 5 in
6 at (BE) / on (AE)

10.5 *Possible answers*
1 Yes, it was very pleasant.
2 I'm going to a meeting.
3 You should take a holiday/vacation.
4 I'm afraid not.
5 It was very hot.
6 Yes, of course. / Yes, certainly.

10.6 2 interesting 3 always 4 arriving in 5 late
6 terrible

10.7 *Possible answers*
1 This is (*name*) from (*company name*). Is that (*name*)?
2 Not too bad. I'd like to arrange a meeting.
3 Are you doing anything on Wednesday? / How about Wednesday?
4 Well, are you free on Thursday? At three o'clock?
5 Good. See you on Thursday at three.

10.8 1 a 2 a 3 b 4 a 5 a 6 c

Barbara Pike is going on a business trip. Listen to her asking a colleague for information about the country and mark the correct answer.

Pike: … And where do you recommend I stay? What's the Welcome Inn like?
Man: It's nice there. It's central and has all the usual business facilities that you'll need.
Pike: Oh, good. So I'll get a room there. Now, what's the best way to get into the city centre from the airport? Should I take a taxi?
Man: Well, you can, but you don't need to. There's an

excellent train service. I think there's a train at least once an hour.

Pike: Mmm… . Can you tell me something about the business hours? I mean, what time are the banks open?
Man: The banks? They open at half past eight and close at four thirty.
Pike: I see. And are they open on Saturday too?
Man: I'm afraid not. And I'd better warn you, the shops close early on Saturday. During the week they're open until half past six, but on Saturdays they close at four.
Pike: At four! Right. Now, what's the weather like at this time of year?
Man: Well, it's usually warm. But last week it was very cold and wet. So don't forget to take an umbrella with you! By the way, when are you going on this trip?
Pike: Oh, not until the middle of next month. The fifteenth, I think.

Unit 11

11.1

1
am	was
is	was
are	were
become	became
begin	began
come	came
do	did
have	had
get	got
go	went
leave	left
say	said
steal	stole
take	took
think	thought

2 2 went 3 got 4 turned 5 began 6 thought 7 was 8 had 9 was

3 1 F 2 B 3 D 4 G 5 A 6 H 7 C 8 E 9 I

Listen to Mr Van der Linde talking about his career and check your answers.

When I left school I went to university. I studied Economics and Business Administration. I finished studying in 1974 and then I got my first job. That was at Unilever. I stayed there for five years. I left in 1979. Then I took a management training course. That lasted for two years. And when I finished that – that was in 1981 – I joined Philips. I worked at Philips for a couple of years, but I really wanted to have my own business. So, I approached the bank, they lent me some money, and two months after I got the loan I left Philips to set up my own business. And I haven't looked back since.

11.2

1 2 HJ 3 HJ 4 DK 5 DK 6 HJ 7 HJ 8 DK

2 *Education:* studied accountancy; trained as a bank clerk; learned French
Work experience: got a job at IBM; worked for ABB; joined JVC
Other information: can speak three languages; has computer skills; can type

3 You meet someone at a party. He tells you about his career, but the party is noisy and you can't hear everything. Listen and ask questions like this:

Voice 1: I joined the company in 19 …
You: (*Beep*) I'm sorry, when did you join the company?
Voice 2: I'm sorry, when did you join the company?

Now you try.

1 V1: I joined the company in 19 …
  (*Beep and pause for response*)
  V2: I'm sorry, when did you join the company?
  (*Beep and pause to repeat*)
  V2: I'm sorry, when did you join the company?

2 V1: At first I worked in the … department.
  (*Beep and pause for response*)
  V2: I'm sorry, which department did you work in?
  (*Beep and pause to repeat*)
  V2: I'm sorry, which department did you work in?

3 V1: My position was … clerk.
  (*Beep and pause for response*)
  V2: I'm sorry, what was your position?
  (*Beep and pause to repeat*)
  V2: I'm sorry, what was your position?

4 V1: I stayed in that job for … years.
  (*Beep and pause for response*)
  V2: I'm sorry, how long did you stay there?
  (*Beep and pause to repeat*)
  V2: I'm sorry, how long did you stay there?

5 V1: I left the company in 19 …
  (*Beep and pause for response*)
  V2: I'm sorry, when did you leave the company?
  (*Beep and pause to repeat*)
  V2: I'm sorry, when did you leave the company?

6 V1: I left because I wanted to …
  (*Beep and pause for response*)
  V2: I'm sorry, why did you leave?
  (*Beep and pause to repeat*)
  V2: I'm sorry, why did you leave?

11.3

1 *Hours:* 1, 3, 8
People: 5, 7, 9
Work: 2, 4, 12
Other: 6, 10, 11

2
1 I worked with interesting people.
2 It was hard work.
3 I learnt a lot.
4 I worked shifts.
5 There was an excellent canteen and a sports club.
6 I did a lot of overtime.

Unit 12

12.1

1 A 23 March   B 5 July   C 01 October
D 11 November

🎧 Listen and write down the dates you hear.
A The trade fair starts on the twenty-third of March.
B I'm flying to Taipei on the fifth of July.
C He joined the company on the first of October.
D The next meeting is on the eleventh of November.

2 🎧 Listen and answer the questions like this:
Voice 1:   When does the trade fair start?
You: (*Beep*) On the second of February.
Voice 2:   On the second of February.

Now you try. Use the dates in the box to answer the questions. The month is the second number!
1 V1: When does the trade fair start?
      (*Beep and pause for response*)
   V2: On the second of February.
      (*Beep and pause to repeat*)
   V2: On the second of February.

2 V1: When are you flying to Taipei?
      (*Beep and pause for response*)
   V2: On the fourth of December.
      (*Beep and pause to repeat*)
   V2: On the fourth of December.

3 V1: When did you join the company?
      (*Beep and pause for response*)
   V2: On the first of January.
      (*Beep and pause to repeat*)
   V2: On the first of January.

4 V1: When are you going on holiday?
      (*Beep and pause for response*)
   V2: On the twenty-second of April.
      (*Beep and pause to repeat*)
   V2: On the twenty-second of April.

3
2 Is there any cheap accommodation near the Centre?
3 Are there any good restaurants near the Centre?
4 Are there any shops near the Centre?
5 Is there any parking near the Centre?
6 Are there any sporting events at the weekend?

2 F   3 D   4 E   5 B   6 C

12.2

1 Hidden words ▼

1 INTERESTED
2 RANGE
3 AVAILABLE
4 DELIVER
5 PRICE
6 INFORMATION
7 STANDARD
8 DISCOUNT
9 BROCHURE

2 🎧 You are at a trade fair. The salesperson is telling you about their new product but the fair is noisy and you can't hear everything. Listen and ask questions like this:

Voice 2: This model costs …
You: (*Beep*) I'm sorry, how much does it cost?
Voice 2: I'm sorry, how much does it cost?
You: (*Beep*) I'm sorry, how much does it cost?
Voice 2: I'm sorry how much does it cost?

Now you try.
1 V1: This model costs …
      (*Beep and pause for response*)
   V2: I'm sorry, how much does it cost?
      (*Beep and pause to repeat*)
   V2: I'm sorry, how much does it cost?

2 V1: It's suitable for …
      (*Beep and pause for response*)
   V2: I'm sorry who's it suitable for?
      (*Beep and pause to repeat*)
   V2: I'm sorry, who's it suitable for?

3 V1: It's available in … sizes.
      (*Beep and pause for response*)
   V2: I'm sorry, what sizes is it available in?
      (*Beep and pause to repeat*)
   V2: I'm sorry, what sizes is it available in?

4 V1: We can deliver in … weeks.
      (*Beep and pause for response*)
   V2: I'm sorry, when can you deliver?
      (*Beep and pause to repeat*)
   V2: I'm sorry, when can you deliver?

12.3

1 1 enclose 2 products 3 stock 4 available
5 contact 6 order

2 1 6 2 No, they aren't. 3 £9.75 4 £895
5 W21 970 054 6 Yes, they are.

3

The **Big** Shirt Company		
45 Duke Street, Edinburgh EH3 6TP		
Customer: Henry Byatt		
Qty	Order Number	Unit Price
50	W21 765 33	9.45
50	W21 765 18	9.45

A customer is placing an order for items from the Big Shirt Company's catalogue. Listen and complete the information on the order form.

This is Henry Byatt ... I'll spell that – B.Y.A.T.T – from Saundersons. I'd like to place an order for some T-shirts. Now, I'd like 50 ... that's five zero ... in blue ... that's catalogue number W21 765 33. And then another 50 in green ... that's catalogue number W21 765 18. I'll repeat that ... 50 T-shirts in blue and 50 in green. Could you send me a written confirmation of the order and let me know when I can expect delivery? Thank you.

Unit 13

13.1

1 2 E 3 B 4 G 5 C 6 H 7 A 8 D
2 1 T 2 F 3 T 4 T 5 T 6 T

13.2

1 cool, cooler, the coolest
fast, faster, the fastest
reliable, more reliable, the most reliable
slow, slower, the slowest
small, smaller, the smallest
successful, more successful, the most successful
ugly, uglier, the ugliest

2 small/large discount
long/short delivery time
high/low price

2 Hobsons has the highest price.
3 Hobsons has the longest delivery time.
4 Office Supply has the lowest price.
5 Office Supply has the largest discount.
6 Office Supply has the best offer.

13.3

1 1 bookcase 2 calendar 3 fax machine
4 filing cabinet 5 map 6 photocopier
7 shelves 8 typewriter

2 *Possible answers*
2 Let's get a filing cabinet.
3 We could buy a clock.
4 I think we should get a map.
5 Let's get a fax machine.
6 We could buy a calendar.

3 You sell office furniture. Practise giving information about prices like this:

Voice 1: How much are the large size desks?
You: (*Beep*) One hundred and twenty-nine pounds.
Voice 2: One hundred and twenty-nine pounds.
You: (*Beep*) One hundred and twenty-nine pounds.
Voice 2: One hundred and twenty-nine pounds.

Now you try. Use the price list in the book to help you.

1 V1: How much are the large size desks?
    (*Beep and pause for response*)
  V2: One hundred and twenty-nine pounds.
    (*Beep and pause to repeat*)
  V2: One hundred and twenty-nine pounds.

2 V1: What do the standard size desks cost?
    (*Beep and pause for response*)
  V2: Ninety-five pounds.
    (*Beep and pause to repeat*)
  V2: Ninety-five pounds.

3 V1: How much are the executive chairs?
    (*Beep and pause for response*)
  V2: A hundred and eighty-three pounds.
    (*Beep and pause to repeat*)
  V2: A hundred and eighty-three pounds.

4 V1: What does the bookcase cost?
    (*Beep and pause for response*)
  V2: Sixty-nine pounds fifty.
    (*Beep and pause to repeat*)
  V2: Sixty-nine pounds fifty.

Unit 14

14.1

1 1 F 2 F 3 T 4 F 5 T
2 1 E 2 D 3 F 4 C 5 A 6 B

3 🔊 Practise asking people questions and answering them.

First, listen and repeat like this:

Voice: Where are you from?
You: *(Beep)* Where are you from?
Voice: Where are you from?

Now you try.

1 V: Where are you from?
   (Beep and pause to repeat)
   V: Where are you from?

2 V: What do you do?
   (Beep and pause to repeat)
   V: What do you do?

3 V: Is it your first visit here?
   (Beep and pause to repeat)
   V: Is it your first visit here?

4 V: Are you interested in sport?
   (Beep and pause to repeat)
   V: Are you interested in sport?

5 V: What sports do you play?
   (Beep and pause to repeat)
   V: What sports do you play?

6 V: Can I get you a drink?
   (Beep and pause to repeat)
   V: Can I get you a drink?

Now listen and answer like this:

Voice 1: Where are you from?
You: *(Beep)* I'm from Melbourne, Australia.
Voice 2: I'm from Melbourne, Australia.

Now you try. You should use your own information!

1 V: Where are you from?
   (Beep and pause for response)

2 V: What do you do?
   (Beep and pause for response)

3 V: Is it your first visit here?
   (Beep and pause for response)

4 V: Are you interested in sport?
   (Beep and pause for response)

5 V: What sports do you play?
   (Beep and pause for response)

6 V: Can I get you a drink?
   (Beep and pause for response)

14.2

1 1 speaking 2 invite 3 kind 4 suit 5 fine
6 forward 7 lunch 8 like 9 sounds 10 exactly
11 make 12 pity

2 *Possible answers*
2 That sounds nice. What time?
3 I'm afraid I'm going to a concert.
4 That's very kind of you. Wednesday's fine.
5 I'm afraid I can't make Thursday. I've got a lot of work.
6 I'd love to.

3
```
Mary Simmons
Bodycare Inc.
111 Park Avenue South
New York, NY 10003              July 10 199-

Dear Mary

Thank you for your letter of July 4 inviting
me to attend the launch of your new range of
Bodycare products. I am pleased to accept
and look forward to seeing you on August 7.

Best regards

janice
```

14.3

1 *Vegetables:* pepper, mushroom, carrot *Fruit:* banana, melon, strawberry, orange, cherry

2 1 Stuffed mushrooms 2 Chicken Kiev 3 coffee

🔊 Listen to this conversation in a restaurant. What does the man order?

Woman: Ah, here's the menu ... now, would you like a starter?
Man: Er, yes. What can you recommend?
Woman: Well, the stuffed mushrooms are usually very good. And so are the prawns.
Man: Stuffed mushrooms. Mmm ... that sounds nice. Yes, I'll have them.
Woman: What would you like for a main course?
Man: What's the Beef Strogonoff like? Is it very hot?
Woman: No, no. It's quite a mild dish. But the sauce is very rich.
Man: Hmm, perhaps I won't have that. I think I'll take the chicken. Yes, Chicken Kiev. I haven't had that for a long time.
Woman: Would you like French fries or rice with it?
Man: Er ... rice, I think.
Man: That was very good. I really enjoyed that.
Woman: Good. ... Now, how about a dessert? A fruit salad perhaps?
Man: Er ... I don't think so. I think I'll just have a coffee, thank you.

Unit 15

15.1 1 left 2 was 3 got 4 joined 5 started 6 sold 7 went 8 came

15.2
1. When did you join the company?
2. What was your position?
3. Which department did you work in?
4. How long did you work (stay) there?
5. Do you have any rooms free?
6. Do you have any T-shirts in stock?

15.3 1 cheaper 2 biggest 3 more expensive 4 better 5 most important 6 fastest

15.4 1 in 2 on 3 in 4 in 5 in 6 for

15.5 *Possible answers*
1. Yes, that sounds nice. / I'm afraid I'm busy on Monday.
2. Yes, I did. It was very interesting.
3. Hold the line. I'll put you through to Ms Chesney.
4. That's a good idea.
5. I'd like chicken, please.

15.7 *Possible answers*
1. Good morning. I'd like some information about your filing cabinets.
2. How much do they cost?
3. Are they available in black?
4. When can you deliver the goods?
5. Thank you for your help.

15.8 1 No: from $75.00   2 No: not grey from stock
3 No: $10   4 Yes: still from $101
5 Yes: black or grey from stock   6 No: $14

Read the information from an office supplier's catalogue. Then listen to a phone conversation between a customer and the supplier. Is the numbered information in the catalogue correct?

Supplier: Office Furniture. Good morning.
Customer: Hello. This is Patricia Exton from Barker and Watson. I'd like some information about office chairs.
Supplier: Right. Er, what exactly would you like to know?
Customer: Well, we need some chairs for our new office. I've got a copy of your catalogue … I'd just like to confirm the details. Now catalogue number 8001 – that's the typist chair?
Supplier: Yes, that's right. It costs from $75.
Customer: $75. Right. And it's available in black and grey from stock?
Supplier: Well, in black, yes, but not in grey; I'm afraid the manufacturers have discontinued it in grey. You see, it wasn't very popular.
Customer: Oh, that's a pity. Well, what about in red?
Supplier: Yes, and we can deliver that from stock.
Customer: Fine. And that costs an extra $9?
Supplier: Er … $10.
Customer: An extra $10. And what about the operator chair? The one with arms. Er … that's catalogue number 3001. Does that still cost from $101?
Supplier: Yes, it does. All colours are available from stock.
Customer: And in red that's an extra $11?
Supplier: I'm afraid not. That should be $14. It sounds to me as if you've got a copy of last year's catalogue. Would you like me to send you a new one?
Customer: Ah, yes, if you would. Thank you very much. Let me give you our address. It's …

Unit 16

16.1

1 1 appointment 2 need 3 could 4 sign 5 of 6 course 7 factory 8 important 9 come 10 else 11 see 12 interesting

2 1 D 2 A 3 B 4 C
1. Don't touch!
2. Be careful!
3. Stand back!
4. Watch out!

16.2

1
buy	bought	bought
come	came	come
do	did	done
get	got	got (BE) / gotten (AE)
go	went	gone
have	had	had
leave	left	left
make	made	made
meet	met	met
put	put	put
say	said	said
see	saw	seen
sell	sold	sold
speak	spoke	spoken
read	read	read
take	took	taken
write	wrote	written

2 2 Have you reserved a hotel room?
3 Have you arranged a meeting with Kruger?
4 Have you changed the meeting with Klonowski?
5 Have you confirmed the meeting with Gruber?
6 Have you cancelled the meeting with Pinkowski?

He has done numbers 1, 2, 4, 5 and 6.

📼 Listen to a conversation between Mr Bly and Mr Cox and tick the things Mr Cox has done.

Bly: Now, Mr Cox, can we just go through the arrangements for my trip to Chicago? Have you booked a flight?
Cox: Yes, I have. You're flying with American Airlines on 23 June. The flight leaves at eight a.m.
Bly: Fine. And what about accommodation? Have you reserved a room at the Plaza?
Cox: I'm afraid I haven't. You see, I couldn't get a room there. They were full up, so I've booked you in at the City Hotel.
Bly: Good. By the way, have you arranged a meeting with Kruger?
Cox: I'm afraid I haven't. I tried to phone him, but he wasn't there. I'll try again tomorrow.
Bly: I see. And what about that meeting with Klonowski? Have you changed the meeting with Klonowski?
Cox: Yes, I have. You're now seeing her when you get back, on June 28.
Bly: That's fine. Have you confirmed the meeting with Gruber?
Cox: Yes, I have. You're seeing him on the twenty-fifth at nine a.m. for breakfast. I'm afraid that's the only time he could make.
Bly: For breakfast. Hmm. Well, I suppose it's better than nothing. ... That's everything, then.
Cox: Er ... you asked me to cancel the meeting with Pinkowski.
Bly: Oh, yes ... well, have you cancelled it?
Cox: But of course!

3 *Possible answers*
1 I've / I haven't been late for work/college.
2 I've / I haven't taken a day off.
3 I've / I haven't gone home early.
4 I've / I haven't spoken English.
5 I've / I haven't written a letter.
6 I've / I haven't made a phone call.

16.3

1 Hidden word ▼

```
1 P R I C E S
2 E Q U I P M E N T
3 P L A N T
4 G R O U P
5 B R A N D
6 S Y S T E M
```

2 2 We've closed the factory in Atlanta.
3 We've started exporting to Japan.
4 We started exporting to Japan last year.
5 We've sold our popcorn business.
6 We've bought a frozen food company.

3 📼 A friend phones you with news of their company. Unfortunately the line is bad and you can't understand everything. Listen and ask questions like this:

Voice 1: We've opened an office in ...
You: (*Beep*) I'm sorry, where have you opened an office?
Voice 2: I'm sorry, where have you opened an office?
You: (*Beep*) I'm sorry, where have you opened an office?
Voice 2: I'm sorry where have you opened an office?

Now you try.

1 V1: We've opened an office in ...
   (*Beep and pause for response*)
   V2: I'm sorry, where have you opened an office?
   (*Beep and pause to repeat*)
   V2: I'm sorry, where have you opened an office?

2 V1: We've closed the factory in ...
   (*Beep and pause for response*)
   V2: I'm sorry, where have you closed the factory?
   (*Beep and pause to repeat*)
   V2: I'm sorry, where have you closed the factory?

3 V1: We've stopped producing ...
   (*Beep and pause for response*)
   V2: I'm sorry, what have you stopped producing?
   (*Beep and pause to repeat*)
   V2: I'm sorry, what have you stopped producing?

4 V1: We've started selling ...
   (*Beep and pause for response*)
   V2: I'm sorry, what have you started selling?
   (*Beep and pause to repeat*)
   V2: I'm sorry, what have you started selling?

5 V1: ... has joined the sales team.
   (*Beep and pause for response*)
   V2: I'm sorry, who's joined the sales team?
   (*Beep and pause to repeat*)
   V2: I'm sorry, who's joined the sales team?

6 V1: ... has left the company.
   (*Beep and pause for response*)
   V2: I'm sorry, who's left the company?
   (*Beep and pause to repeat*)
   V2: I'm sorry, who's left the company?

Unit 17

17.1

1 *Transport:* subway, car, bus, tram
Entertainment: show, concert, play, jazz
Scenery: park, lake, beach, coast

2 1 b 2 c 3 b 4 a 5 a

17.2

1 🔊 Practise offering to do things. Listen and repeat the offers like this:

Voice: Would you like me to book a hotel?
You: (Beep) Would you like me to book a hotel?
Voice: Would you like me to book a hotel?

Now you try.

1. V: Would you like me to book a hotel?
   (Beep and pause to repeat)
   V: Would you like me to book a hotel?

2. V: Would you like me to meet you at the airport?
   (Beep and pause to repeat)
   V: Would you like me to meet you at the airport?

3. V: Shall I find out about sightseeing tours?
   (Beep and pause to repeat)
   V: Shall I find out about sightseeing tours?

4. V: Shall I reserve a table for this evening?
   (Beep and pause to repeat)
   V: Shall I reserve a table for this evening?

5. V: Do you want me to pick you up at your hotel?
   (Beep and pause to repeat)
   V: Do you want me to pick you up at your hotel?

6. V: Do you want me to call a cab?
   (Beep and pause to repeat)
   V: Do you want me to call a cab?

2 1 B 2 D 3 E 4 C 5 F 6 A

1. £8.50.
2. Midnight.
3. The Barber of Seville.
4. 071 836 2132.
5. 18 August
6. two o'clock.

17.3

1 *Possible answers*
1. I'm afraid I must go.
2. We must have another game soon.
3. That was a lovely meal.
4. Give my regards to Beatrix.

2 1 F 2 F 3 T 4 F 5 T 6 F

🔊 Listen to Ritva Forslund talking to a colleague about a recent trip to Milan. Write true [T] or false [F] for each sentence.

Coll: Morning, Ritva. How did you get on in Milan then?
Ritva: Oh, not too bad at all. I had a look round their new R and D centre, met all the engineers. It was quite impressive, really.
Coll: Did you talk to Taffarello?
Ritva: Yes, we had a meeting with her on Thursday. That was pretty tough – it went on most of the day. But I think it went OK … and then we had dinner together in the evening. There are some nice restaurants in Milan.
Coll: What did you do at the weekend?
Ritva: Well, Nanini looked after me pretty well. He had tickets for the opera on Friday. You know, the Scala. I'm not really an opera fan, but that was quite an experience!
Coll: Did you see any football on Saturday?
Ritva: You bet. AC Milan against Inter-Milan. Great match.
Coll: Who won?
Ritva: No-one. It was a two-two draw.
Coll: It sounds as if you had a good time. Do you think we'll get the contract?
Ritva: I hope so! Nanini's coming here in August for further talks, so we'll see then.

3

Vittorio Nanini
Via San Martino 32
201 46 Milan
Italy   1 July 199-

Dear Mr Nanini

I am writing to thank you for your hospitality while I was in Milan. I had a very enjoyable time and I think the negotiations were very good for both our companies.

Thank you again, and I look forward to seeing you in Helsinki in August.

Yours sincerely

Ritva Forslund
Ritva Forslund

Unit 18

18.1

1 🔊 You will hear someone talking about a problem. Offer to help by phoning the correct department like this:

Voice 1: We need some more envelopes.
You: (Beep) I'll phone the Purchasing Department.
Voice 2: I'll phone the Purchasing Department.
You: (Beep) I'll phone the Purchasing Department.
Voice 2: I'll phone the Purchasing Department.

Now you try.

1. V1: We need some more envelopes.
   (Beep and pause for response)
   V2: I'll phone the Purchasing Department.
   (Beep and pause to repeat)
   V2: I'll phone the Purchasing Department.

2 V1: This invoice is too high.
   (*Beep and pause for response*)
   V2: I'll phone the Accounts Department.
   (*Beep and pause to repeat*)
   V2: I'll phone the Accounts Department.

3 V1: The photocopier's broken down again.
   (*Beep and pause for response*)
   V2: I'll call the Service Department.
   (*Beep and pause to repeat*)
   V2: I'll call the Service Department.

4 V1: I need some information about the new English courses.
   (*Beep and pause for response*)
   V2: I'll call the Personnel Department.
   (*Beep and pause to repeat*)
   V2: I'll call the Personnel Department.

2 A I'll put; I'll try
   B I'll give
   C Are you doing; I'll check; I'm going

3 1 D   2 F   3 B   4 E   5 A   6 C

18.2

1

> Phone message
> From: Mr Ranjit Singh
> Of: GCI
> Phone: 266 3188
> Message: *Please phone back about his order for ballpoint pens, order number H 94 945, before 4 p.m.*

 Listen to this recorded phone call and complete the message.

Good afternoon. My name is Ranjit Singh, that's R.A.N.J.I.T, Ranjit, S.I.N.G.H, Singh, and I'm from GCI. I'm calling about my order for ballpoint pens with our company logo. I ordered five boxes, but you've only sent three. Could you please let me know what's happened to the others? The order number is H 94 945 and you can call me on 266 3188. I'll be in my office until four o'clock.

2 1 calling/phoning/ringing   2 seems
   3 mistake / mix up   4 ordered   5 sent   6 order
   7 line   8 check   9 sorry   10 problems   11 refund
   12 delivery

3 1 problems   2 products   3 apologize
   4 manufacturers   5 orders   6 customers

18.3

1 Hidden word ▼

	1	C	A	N	C	E	L	
2	A	P	O	L	O	G	I	Z	E
3	D	A	M	A	G	E
4	R	E	P	L	A	C	E
5	D	E	L	A	Y
6	R	E	P	A	I	R
7	M	I	S	T	A	K	E
8	R	E	F	U	N	D

2 None of the above.

3 *Possible answer*

> **Avalon Industries**
> 28 Devonport Rd
> Stoke
> Plymouth PL3 4DW
> England
>
> Mr Olsen
> Pacific Machines
> 212 Twin Dolphin Drive
> Redwood City CA 94065
>
> 15 August 199-
>
> Dear Mr Olsen
>
> Thank you for your letter of 10 August regarding our order no. AS 671.
>
> I am afraid the fax we sent on 24 July was a mistake and the machine was damaged when we unpacked it.
>
> Would you please send a technician to examine the machine as soon as possible. If it cannot be repaired, we will need a replacement.
>
> I look forward to hearing from you.
>
> Yours sincerely
>
> *B. Rogers*
>
> B Rogers

Unit 19

19.1

1 1 ↑   2 ↓   3 ↓   4 ↓   5 ↑   6 ↑

2 *Possible answers*
   2 Unemployment will go down slightly.
   3 Wages will go up steadily.
   4 Interest rates will rise slightly.
   5 Inflation will fall rapidly.
   6 House prices will decrease dramatically.

3 1 ↑   2 ↑   3 ↑   4 ↑   5 ↑   6 ↑

19.2

1

100%	75%	50%	25%	0%
1, 4	6, 8	5, 9	2, 10	3, 7

2 🔊 Listen to different people's opinions about these predictions, and repeat like this:

Voice 1: I don't think people'll spend their evenings in bars.
You: (Beep) I don't think people'll spend their evenings in bars.
Voice 1: I don't think people'll spend their evenings in bars.

Now you try.

1 V1: I don't think people'll spend their evenings in bars.
   (Beep and pause to repeat)
   V1: I don't think people'll spend their evenings in bars.

2 V2: I expect people'll spend their evenings at home.
   (Beep and pause to repeat)
   V2: I expect people'll spend their evenings at home.

3 V1: I'm sure travel won't be a luxury item.
   (Beep and pause to repeat)
   V1: I'm sure travel won't be a luxury item.

4 V3: I'm certain the working week'll be shorter.
   (Beep and pause to repeat)
   V3: I'm certain the working week'll be shorter.

19.3

1 1 computer, modem, fax
      2 A F   B F   C T   D F

2 1 F   2 F   3 F   4 T   5 T   6 T

🔊 Listen to this man talking about telecommuting. Write true [T] or false [F] for each sentence.

I started working from home a couple of years ago. Er ... the first thing I found was that my working week became much shorter ... er ... when I was in London I would work from nine in the morning until seven at night and then I came down here and found I was doing the same work in two or three hours. The main reason was that I didn't have to bother about the staff of my holiday company. You see, I became the company's only employee; the rest of the company went freelance. Take my secretary, for example. She moved to Ireland, bought a house and doubled her salary by working for several bosses instead of one. So, you see, I think telecommuting is a good thing. I'd recommend it to anyone.

Unit 20

20.1 1 rose   2 fell   3 went   4 declined   5 tried
         6 stopped   7 started   8 was   9 has not been
         10 have begun   11 have fallen   12 has cut

20.2 1 Yes, I have.
          2 No, they didn't.
          3 Yes, they will.
          4 Yes, they did.
          5 No, they won't.
          6 No, he/she hasn't.

20.3 1 by   2 from   3 at   4 in   5 in   6 of

20.4 *Possible answers*
          1 You're welcome. / It was a pleasure.
          2 I'll call the service department.
          3 That's very kind of you.
          4 I'll phone the sales department.
          5 Thank you. That was very interesting.
          6 Thank you. I will.

20.5 *Entertainment:* museum, theatre, restaurant
          Trends: increase, fall, decline
          Business information: production, wages, inflation
          Company report: sales, equipment

20.6 Bombay: 54c   Singapore: 99c
          Jakarta: 33c   Tokyo: 43c
          Bangkok: 23c   Sydney: 50c
          Kuala Lumpur: 48c

🔊 Look at the graph comparing the price of an average bag of potato chips in different countries in South East Asia. Some prices in the graph are wrong. Listen to the tape and correct them.

Potato chips around the world

Are you a potato chip fan? Do you just love eating bags and bags of chips? Are you paying too much in your country? Where is the best place for you to buy your favourite food? We've done a study on the price of potato chips in seven different countries around the Asia–Pacific area. All the following prices are in US dollars and cents.

If you live in Singapore, we suggest you move to Jakarta or Bangkok. In Singapore the average price of a bag of potato chips is 99 cents; in Jakarta, you'll pay 33 cents and in Bangkok only 23 cents. It's surprising, but a bag of chips in Kuala Lumpur is more expensive than in Tokyo. People in Kuala Lumpur pay an average 48 cents whereas the Japanese pay five cents less per bag – 43 cents. In Bombay you'll pay slightly more for your potato chips than in Sydney: 54 cents in Bombay and 50 cents in Sydney.